Making Every Six Minutes Count

CATRIN MILLS

Head of events and books
Leah Darbyshire

Commissioning editor
Laura Slater

Editorial assistant
Edward Bowes

Published by
Globe Law and Business Ltd
3 Mylor Close
Horsell
Woking
Surrey GU21 4DD
United Kingdom
Tel: +44 20 3745 4770
www.globelawandbusiness.com

ISBN: 978-1-78358-266-2
A catalogue record for this book is available from the British Library

Contents

Foreword

It's not a coincidence that I'm writing a book about time management at possibly the busiest time in my entire life.

In the last four years I've built a division in a law firm, got married, moved house, had two children, re-trained as a coach, and started my own business. When I was asked to write a book about time management, I didn't fail to see the irony – my first thought was how am I going to find the time to do that?

But that's precisely the point. There is a perception that anyone who professes to know about time management must lead a serene existence and have plenty of spare time to do nothing. This is possibly why lawyers find the whole topic alien. For many, it has the image of a 'touchy feely' subject which boils down to applying a bit of common sense. Such subjects do not sit comfortably with busy legal professionals.

But time management is not about doing less. It's not even about being more organised (although personal organisation enables you to manage your time well). It's being selective about what you do and enabling you to do more of what is of value to you – things which make you fulfilled, successful, and happy. In essence, it's about enabling you to achieve your ambitions and realise your goals.

The other great irony about this report is that you will need it most at times when you feel the last thing you have time to do is read it. A comment I often come across is, 'Surely spending time learning about time management is, in itself, a waste of time?'

It was relatively late in my legal career that I began to read about time management and I had those very same thoughts. I was sceptical about how much time management literature could teach lawyers, who are trained to be incisive and analytical. 'Surely', I thought, 'Managing your time is all about being sensible, making a list, and then getting your head down?' A degree of stress is positively cultivated in the legal profession, and deadlines and late nights are considered the norm, so I wasn't sure that time management held any answers for the state of the legal profession. But, as soon as I started to read, I discovered keys and techniques which had taken me over 10 years to work out.

There are many lawyers who struggle with heavy workloads, competing demands, and conflicting pressures, but as they have no idea how to tackle these issues, their situation inevitably becomes worse. They end up more stressed and less productive.

Time management is not all obvious but much of it is simple to master. Simply adopting a few easy practices can free up valuable time. This makes you instantly less stressed and more successful – not just in your work, but in all areas of your life.

There is over 30 years' worth of literature on the concept of time management applying to the business world generally. Law is a world unto itself. As a lawyer, you don't have the time to trawl through books written for other sectors which don't understand the specific demands and requirements of the legal profession. In writing this book, I have taken into consideration the day-to-day challenges facing lawyers when applying the time management techniques, so that you can make better use of your time – the key to being a happier and more successful legal practitioner.

Executive summary

Time is a lawyer's commodity – or rather – it is how most lawyers quantify their expertise. How successful you are as a lawyer depends fundamentally on how you use your time. There is a direct correlation between how much value you can extract from your time and your profitability. Most lawyers must record how they spend their time on a daily basis and regularly justify their use of time to clients, the court, or their employers.

Since time is a concept at the heart of the legal profession, why is it that very few lawyers seriously think about time management? Little formal training is available to lawyers on time management, and few lawyers really think about or plan how they allocate their time, let alone analyse what they get out of it. Many lawyers assume that time management is something they already grasp – that it is something they do intrinsically – and so they assume that there is really nothing to learn.

Making Every Six Minutes Count explains why lawyers should look more objectively at how they spend their time, and how principles of time management can make an enormous difference in a profession which is now at its most stressful and intensive. The more efficiently and effectively you use your time, the more successful your practice will be. But this book is about more than ensuring profitability for your practice – although this is a direct consequence of effective time management – it's about bringing you success in the rest of your life, too. Good time management means taking control of your time and achieving professional success while restoring work-life balance. This report guides lawyers in how to make the most of their time both professionally and personally.

Chapter 1 defines time management and its relevancy to lawyers. We deduce that, technically, there is no such thing as time management – what we're really talking about is self management. It is not possible to move, change, or extend time. Time is a constant. This chapter explains how mastering time management really means being able to manage your own activities and actions better. It challenges the perception amongst lawyers that time management, as one of the so-called softer skills, is something they don't need training in, but learning about time management is a small investment for a big return.

Before you can address your working habits and behaviours, it is helpful to straighten out your working area so as to make it conducive to effective time management. Chapter 2 addresses lawyers' obsession with hard copies and provides practical advice on how to eliminate unnecessary paperwork, how to organise diaries, to-do lists, schedules, and contacts, and how to streamline your office to allow you to see things more clearly.

Chapter 3 highlights the importance of planning. Lawyers are taught how to plan cases, yet they typically spend very little time planning their working hours. In this chapter, we look at how a small amount of planning can mean an effective working strategy. We look at the difference between time management and time leadership, and how planning your time also involves keeping an eye on the bigger picture.

Chapter 4 turns to the art of prioritising. It includes basic tools to help you prioritise your tasks. We also examine how to use prioritisation to deal with overwhelm and the feeling of dread when faced with too much to do. The concept of the 'to-day' list is also introduced here.

Delegation is the single, most effective way to instantly win more time. Chapter 5 examines the skills needed to delegate effectively.

Chapter 6 addresses the issue of procrastination – a principal reason why lawyers lose much time during the working day. It provides some practical tips on how to overcome procrastination and recognise the black holes into which time easily disappears.

We now live in a society where we are constantly reachable. But this also means we are constantly interruptible. Chapter 7 examines how to deal with communications and interruptions. It provides advice on dealing with common distractions such as email, the internet, the phone, and even personal interruptions from friends and colleagues.

Chapter 8 takes the concept of time and self management further by discussing how to be proactive instead of reactive. We discuss how to set boundaries for yourself and how to say 'no'. This chapter also introduces the concept of work-life balance and explains why it is elusive for lawyers.

Managing time effectively means managing clients effectively. Chapter 9 examines how ineffective client management leads to significant amounts of wasted time, impacting negatively on the level of service provided. It also contains advice on managing clients more proactively to provide an ideal service.

Chapter 10 examines the difficulty faced by many lawyers in finding time for business development. This chapter offers useful advice on how to fit in marketing and networking, and how to identify the 'quick wins' and get the most marketing mileage for the least amount of time.

With rising numbers of lawyers seeking help for mental health issues such as depression, anxiety, stress, and ultimately breakdown, Chapter 11 analyses how stress has affected the legal profession and the importance of protecting lawyers' mental wellbeing.

Chapter 12 focuses on how you can use time management to attain professional and personal success and fulfilment. Developing the theme of personal development and career planning in previous chapters, this chapter explains how you can closely align time management with your lifelong goals. While good time management will bring you success and organisation on a day-to-day level, as the days add up to weeks, months, and years, how can you ensure that your investment is bringing you closer to achieving your ambitions?

Finally, Chapter 13 provides real-life accounts of the time management challenges faced by lawyers, from trainees to managing partners. A broad range of lawyers have been interviewed to show that time management is an issue common to all in the profession. But some lawyers who have mastered time management are using it to their advantage, and their accounts reveal how.

About the author

Catrin Mills trained as a solicitor with City firm Reynolds Porter Chamberlain, where she spent five years as an employment lawyer before moving to a regional firm to set up her own employment department. In 2009, Catrin took a short career break during which she provided coaching and mentoring to other solicitors and wrote two books on personal development for lawyers, including this one. Catrin then returned to private practice, joining Longmores Solicitors, where she is now a partner and head of the firm's Harlow office. Catrin advises on all aspects of HR and employment law.

Acknowledgements

I would like to thank Anna Shaw for finding the blog and seeing its potential, and Stephanie Ramasamy for her help and patience in the editing process.

I would also like to thank Heather Townsend (also known as the 'The Efficiency Coach') for her time and wisdom, Jessica Chivers for her enthusiasm and practical advice, my great friend and lawyer Madeline Seibert and her colleague Sheenagh Parsons at Attwaters, and my online networking friends and colleagues, all of whom helped me through the research and writing process of this book.

I'd also like to thank the irrepressible June Cory who didn't laugh when I told her my first business ideas, but who encouraged and helped me to get online, and who has been a constant support ever since.

Chapter 1: Time management – Why bother?

'Time is what we want most, but what we use worst.'

William Penn

Time management is how we describe a set of skills and tools which enable us to allocate our time better. It sounds simple. Time management is really just a case of using your time for the best possible results. This is maybe why many lawyers believe it's a discipline they don't need to learn. It is surely something they must already instinctively know how to do.

Time management is not just as straightforward as making a to-do list, but when you master the basics, you are guaranteed to improve your productivity and achieve more with your time. Time management is not just about being more organised – it's about valuing your time and achieving more with it. Surely this is worth looking into even for busy lawyers – or especially for busy lawyers.

Managing time is managing yourself

First, time management is a meaningless phrase. You can't manage time itself – you can't move it, change it, lengthen it, or delay it. Time is a constant, finite resource. When you run out of it, you can't buy more.

Time is also an equaliser. We all have the same amount – the same 24 hours in a day and 168 hours in every week. What distinguishes us all is what we do with it.

Time management is therefore about managing yourself. It involves self-awareness and it means making changes

– sometimes significant changes – to work and personal behaviours. It involves examining your working practices, changing your environment, and altering habits which may have been with you for years. Often, time management means changing the way you think about your work, your goals, your ambitions and, even your life generally. It can also mean changes in the way you interact with others.

Applying time management tools can bring powerful and life-changing results. The bottom line is, time management will not only make you more successful, but it will make you more fulfilled.

A busy lawyer is not necessarily a successful lawyer

Law is undoubtedly one of the busiest professions. Being a lawyer means constantly coping with competing demands. Lawyers must juggle professional demands from their clients, courts, colleagues, and even opponents. Being a lawyer means keeping your clients informed while meeting strict deadlines. It means being constantly available while progressing professional matters swiftly. It means being able to wear different hats and to interchange them seamlessly. Lawyers often have to be accountants, PR executives, marketing experts, human resource managers, financial controllers, counsellors, and at the same time, keep up with the law.

What's more, making a living as a lawyer means doing all of this within the confines of professional regulatory requirements and billing targets. Being a successful lawyer, therefore, depends on a very high level of efficiency. While being a lawyer means inevitably being busy, being a successful lawyer means being busy and effective – and there's a big difference between the two. Achieving success as a lawyer means ensuring that you are busying yourself in the right way, and focusing on the important areas. This will be explored further in this book.

Avoiding the vicious circle

In today's world, personal time management is as important as professional time management. With many lawyers suffering from stress and its associated problems such as anxiety, depression, exhaustion, physical illnesses, alcohol or drug addiction, and relationship problems, it is important to develop skills to maintain a balance between life and work, and to ensure that time outside work is devoted to your personal wellbeing.

Being a lawyer is not just a job, it is a professional vocation – it is a way of life. If you are to succeed in law, it is vital that you are equipped with the tools not just to function, but to excel under the intense pressure which comes with the territory.

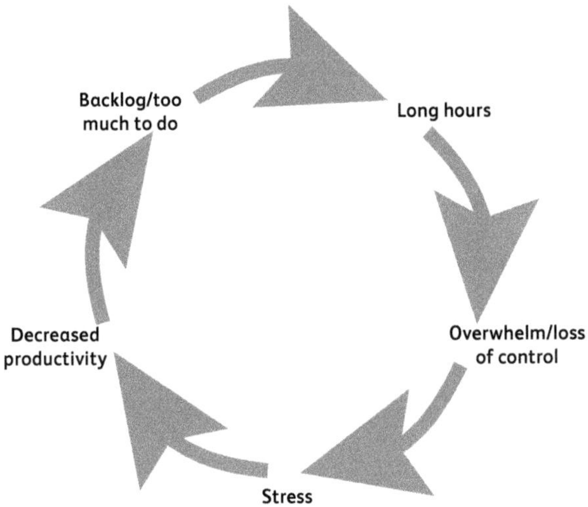

Figure 1: The vicious circle

Many lawyers struggle in a vicious circle which can be likened to Figure 1. Being overwhelmed with work means you stay late in the office. Working longer hours makes you exhausted and stressed which, in turn, makes you less productive. Lower productivity creates a bigger workload and so it continues.

Time management can help you create and exist in a virtuous circle like that illustrated in Figure 2. Being in control of your time makes you less stressed and able to work more productively. This leaves you time to have more of a balance in life which helps maintain perspective and, in turn, keep things under control. In fact, these things are so interlinked that you could rearrange the words in the circles in Figure 2 and still end up with the same result.

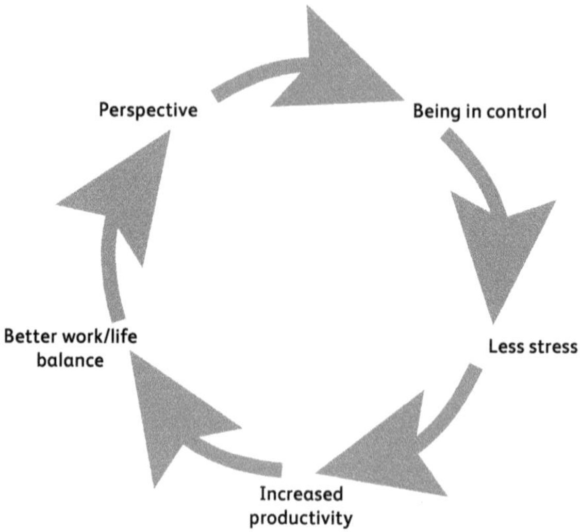

Figure 2: The virtuous circle

How this book can help you

The fact that you are reading this book suggests that you already recognise that time is an issue. Perhaps you are feeling overwhelmed with your workload, or feel overburdened with the stress of having too much to do in too little time. You can change all of this relatively quickly and easily. This book will show you how to adapt the way you approach work and your life generally, to ensure that you are making the most of all of your time and to help you eradicate all of those traps where your time is being wasted. In particular, you can expect to achieve the following.

Increased productivity

By ensuring that you are spending your time in the most effective way, it stands to reason that your productivity will increase. You will be able to do more in less time and you will be focusing on those tasks which are important, instead of wasting valuable time on tasks which are unnecessary, irrelevant, or serve no purpose.

Greater success

Knowing that you are spending your time effectively, and in accordance with a broader plan, means that all of your actions have integrity. Having confidence in how you spend your time gives you a feeling of purpose and empowerment. This confidence propels you forward to achieve greater things.

Better work-life balance

Many lawyers may well laugh out loud if you ask them whether they have work-life balance. It is a phrase which has no place in many lawyers' vocabularies. What this book aims to show is that it is possible – and in fact essential – that lawyers address the massive imbalance which currently exists in their lives. Learning time management will allow you to achieve a work-life balance and be a more successful lawyer. The former need not be at the cost of the latter.

Better overall health

Stress is epidemic amongst members of the legal profession. Mastering time management means being in control of your work and your life. It therefore means reducing and ultimately eliminating stress. As the number of lawyers suffering from stress and other related illnesses soars, learning to manage yourself better will enable you to protect yourself against the ill-health affecting a significant proportion of the profession. Staying healthy and looking after yourself means you have more energy and are more efficient.

There are many different types of lawyers, from international magic-circle partners to sole practitioners, from in-house legal teams to public sector advisers, from corporate or commercial specialists to litigators, and from trainees to managing principals.

This book does not attempt to offer one solution which will fit all. However, there are time challenges which are common to all lawyers. What this book provides is suggestions on how to make better use of your time, whatever your area of practice. It must, of course, be read in the context of whatever jurisdictional or regulatory rules apply to you and it is certainly not intended to override or contradict practice rules or legal requirements. What it does offer is insight into how you can make better use of your time, to serve your clients – and yourself – more effectively.

Chapter 2:
Start with your environment

'A man is not idle because he is absorbed in thought. There is a visible labour and there is an invisible labour.'

Victor Hugo

Before you can start to think about how you spend your time and how you can do this better, you need to go back to basics. It is impossible to step back and examine how you can improve your time management unless your environment is geared up for that.

Get some clarity

If a cluttered desk is a cluttered mind, then surely that means an empty desk means an empty mind. The person who said this must have been a lawyer. This statement sums up a mindset which holds many lawyers back, and that is assuming that surrounding themselves with lots of paper makes them busy, valuable, important, or more efficient. A clear desk does not mean lack of work or an absent caseload. A clear desk means clarity of thought and action.

Clear up

De-cluttering is not the exclusive domain of annoying home-makeover shows. In law school, one of the first things you learn is when seeing a client, all files relating to other clients should be put away. It's a very basic client confidentiality issue. You wouldn't expect to visit a doctor and see someone else's medical notes lying around.

These days, the majority of lawyers don't see clients in their own offices, but it's still a good practice to get into. As any lawyer who has sent a letter to a client with the wrong enclosures will tell you, operating in a state of disarray can lead to embarrassing mix-ups and unnecessary mistakes. Worse still, trying to work amongst a pile of paperwork means wasted time, and lots of it.

Time spent shuffling papers for no reason, moving files around as you try to find something you've lost (usually your pen), shifting piles of papers from one side of your desk to the other as you decide which you're going to work on first, or tidying your papers as a distraction to avoid an unpleasant task or phone call, are all a complete waste of your time and could be avoided if you had a clear desk.

Clinging on to files

It's fascinating how many lawyers seem to cocoon themselves in a filing fortress. Is it a form of security blanket? Does it help them concentrate? Are they quite literally submerging themselves in their work? I'm sure such habits would yield plenty of psychoanalysis material, but as a manager, I would despair if employees say things like, 'But this is just how I work' or 'I know it looks a mess but I know where everything is'. While some commentators might say that it is perfectly acceptable for people to have different ways of working, and to an extent I would agree, I would go out on a limb here and say that such statements simply betray complete and utter delusion. Lawyers who operate in chaos are functioning despite it.

All of us know lawyers who use their desk as a to-do list and who become instantly fretful at any suggestion that they might put the files in the filing cabinet, for which it was designed. They worry that if something is out of sight, it is out of mind. But if you are worried about forgetting something, the answer is not to have all your files within arm's reach. You need to improve your system for scheduling tasks and deadlines. Making sure all of your files are within grabbing distance won't help you remember things, it's a visual distraction which stops you focusing, and which will just make you feel overwhelmed.

Most lawyers will at least have a diary, and many law firms now have case management systems which allow for the scheduling of tasks on your computer. Keep a list or diary note of what needs to be done on files and then put the files away until you intend to address those tasks. If the files sit on your desk, each time you see them you'll waste precious time worrying about what you have to do on them next week, instead of focusing on what you need to do today.

Ditch the paperwork

Being surrounded by unnecessary papers and documents is not just harmful for the environment, it's distracting and inefficient. I'm sure there is a joke to be made about saving rainforests and being able to see the wood for the trees, but I've yet to find it.

I worked at a firm which was on a very brave mission to become paperless. It was interesting to see how much resistance it experienced. There is a certain characteristic inherent in lawyers which makes them very anxious about letting go of hard copies. In today's world though, there is no excuse for not using technology to help you be more efficient.

Ask yourself these types of questions regularly:

- Do I really need to print that email?
- Am I creating correspondence for the sake of it?
- Can I send an email or make a phone call instead of sending a letter?
- Do I really need a hard copy (or several copies) of that document on the file? and
- Will it suffice to save that note on the system instead of printing it?

Of course, firms vary in the technology available, and I'm

not for one moment suggesting that you compromise on the stringent record keeping which must be adhered to, but if the mechanisms for reducing paperwork are there – use them. If, for example, your case history is saved electronically, do you really need to keep a hard copy of everything?

In some firms, the technology won't be available to the same extent. However, if your practice is to work from hard copy files, do you need four copies of the same draft?

A word on filing

As a junior lawyer I was fortunate to work with some great legal secretaries and I learned a lot from them, including that the bane of their lives was filing. How often have you heard someone ask 'Where's the letter we sent yesterday?' and the response, 'Oh, it's in filing', as if filing were a place. Some lawyers had filing systems for their filing – an exercise in tautology, surely?

I have to admit, I still struggle to understand how filing becomes a task in itself. If there is filing which needs doing, doesn't this just mean that the paperwork has got out of hand? Isn't filing just another word for a pile of papers in the wrong place? For solicitors who are fortunate enough to have secretaries, this should be something which is done magically. For others, do it as you go along while you're working on the file.

For the avoidance of any doubt, filing goes in files. Your in-tray, desk, spare office chair, or office floor are not where your filing should be – if there is a piece of paper which doesn't belong in any file, then it's destined for the green file (the recycling bin). A good test to have in mind when sorting paperwork is not 'might I need this again?' but 'can I get this information somewhere else if I ever need it?'

There is a school of thought which says that for high-order efficiency, you should only touch a piece of paper once. When you've read it, action it, then file it or bin it. This might be a bit of a tall order for lawyers, but the principle is a good one.

The single-file rule

Have just one file on your desk at a time – the file you're working on. How many times have you started your day this way, but been interrupted by a call on another file, so you reach the end of the day with a stack of open files in front of you as one has overtaken the other in priority. The solution to this is to take the call, do your note, diary an action, and put the file back. Go back to the task in hand. If you're constantly interrupted on a big task, consider taking yourself away from the phone to do it. (For more tips on dealing with interruptions, see Chapter 7.)

Using diaries and schedules

I am assuming that all lawyers have some sort of diary. If you are a lawyer and you don't have a diary, I don't know how you are doing it.

For most lawyers, deadlines are crucial. You should have systems in place for noting deadlines such as limitation dates, completion or court deadlines, hearing dates, etc. Aside from time management considerations, there are important risk management considerations when it comes to recording deadlines. Having an effective system for noting and keeping deadlines is one of the fundamentally important systems you should have in place.

For these and other appointments or tasks, some people use a paper diary or some use a diary on their computer. If you are IT literate you might have an office computer diary linked to a BlackBerry or similar device. Whatever method you use, have just one diary instead of several. Record work and personal appointments in the same place to avoid clashes, and to save time having to keep and check more than one schedule.

The simpler your diary system, the easier it will be to use and the more effective it will be. The whole point is that you have one place to record all appointments or anything which relates to how you are going to spend your time. Say goodbye, therefore, to post-it notes or scraps of paper reminding you that you are due at the opticians at 2pm and that you need to be home on time because your friends are coming over for dinner. Bits of paper get lost and you waste time reading all the other bits of paper before you get to the one you need. Have everything in one place, and whenever you need to make a note of an appointment, important task, or event, write it down where it should be.

Contact information

I am always amused to see how many lawyers still work on computers which have a sort of fringe-like edging made up of adhesive notes bearing telephone numbers – your secretary's extension number, your manager's extension number, your fax number in case anyone asks for it, etc. Inevitably, they fall off or you can't find them. Have one database of contact numbers. Whenever you need a number it will always be in the same place. Some firms have an intranet which will give you colleagues' numbers. Why duplicate things by writing down information which is already on your computer?

Whenever anyone gives you their contact details, don't write them on a scrap of paper. Enter them directly into your contacts database.

Business cards

Keep these all in one place until you've entered the contact details onto your database. A good tip is to make a note on the back of when and where you met the person. Once the information has been transferred, file cards away in a rolodex or similar. Better still, delegate all of this to your secretary if you have one. What you want to avoid is an array of business cards, scraps of paper, or sticky notes littered across your desk.

Journals and know-how

The amount of information lawyers have to keep on top of is inordinate. You can easily end up with at least three or four journals hitting your desk each week, not to mention monthly briefings, email newsletters, etc. (For tips on dealing with incoming emails, see Chapter 7.)

If your office is a dumping ground for journals, you need a reading pile. Put all journals you plan to read in the same place and, whenever you have an opportunity, take one with you to read. Weed out the pile regularly – anything that has been there over six months, get rid of it. If you receive hard-copy journals as part of a circulation list, flick through, photocopy what's of interest, then pass them on to your colleagues. Hanging on to journals without reading them is depriving others of the resource.

Hopefully having read this chapter, you have now minimised your paperwork so that you have a clear platform from which to start the real time-management work.

Chapter 3: **Planning**

'To begin with the end in mind means to start with a clear understanding of your destination. It means to know where you're going so that you better understand where you are now and so that the steps you take are always in the right direction. It's incredibly easy to get caught up in an activity trap, in the busy-ness of life, to work harder and harder at climbing the ladder of success only to discover it's leaning against the wrong wall. It is possible to be busy – very busy – without being very effective.'

Stephen R. Covey[1]

So important is the concept of planning that it forms one of the seven keys to effectiveness according to Stephen R. Covey in his work *The 7 Habits of Highly Effective People.* His rule is simple – begin with the end in mind.

There are different levels of planning – planning your morning, your day, your week, the next six months, the year ahead, and even your career and your life. There is more on broader and long-term planning in Chapter 12, but first, let's look at planning on a day-to-day level.

It's not real work

Planning, like time management generally, is something all

lawyers believe is easy, but if that's the case, why aren't more lawyers doing it? Is it because they see it as an unnecessary time-waster, preventing them starting their 'real' work?

In training, lawyers are taught to develop case plans although, in practice, many don't, and few start the day by drawing up a plan of how they intend to spend their time. Instead, many lawyers are constantly caught up in the frenzy of day-to-day activity.

Typically, you start the day feeling already overwhelmed because you have so much to do. You don't know where to begin so you just take a deep breath and dive head first into the pile on your desk. You spend your day flailing about, trying to do more than one thing at once, hoping that something will somehow get accomplished by the end of the day.

In your anxiety to plough through the work, you don't stop to think if what you're doing is necessary or important, or to consider why you're doing it in the first place. By the end of the day, you realise that eight hours have passed and you have barely looked up from your desk all day. The pile on your desk seems even bigger than it was that morning and, although you've slaved all day long, skipped lunch, and cancelled coffee with your good friend, you can't for the life of you think of one thing you've actually achieved. You go home feeling more exhausted and depressed, dreading returning to work the next morning. Day by day you grow more exhausted and stressed and less able to muster the energy to launch another attack on your growing workload.

The problem is this, under huge pressure to clock up billable hours, there is an ingrained discomfort in lawyers about doing anything non-chargeable, let alone anything as basic as making a plan of how you intend to spend your morning. On top of this, lawyers are driven by an instinct to start shovelling through the work in order to quieten the mental interference of impending deadlines and chasing clients. Here are some examples of where this type of approach can lead you:

- There's that lengthy witness statement which you spent hours on, but which turned out to be irrelevant to the issues in the case, so all your time was written off the final bill;
- You might have spent a whole day drafting a legal essay explaining to your client with forensic reference to case law why they don't have a case, only to have to spend almost the same amount of time with them on the phone explaining your advice in plain English; or
- You spent most of the morning marking up a draft contract with comments, but a revised version was circulated just before you hit 'send'. You didn't read the original email which warned you of this and so you have to start all over again.

In an occupation where survival depends on billable time, not recorded time – which are two very different things – it is crucial not to spend your time being very busy but ineffective – or in lawyer terms, carrying out work which you won't get paid for and serves no other purpose. In short, effort expended does not equal effectiveness.

It's about time leadership

It is entirely possible to be over-occupied but to 'do nothing'. Covey uses an interesting illustration when explaining the difference between management and leadership: 'Management is efficiency in climbing the ladder of success; leadership determines whether the ladder is leaning against the right wall.'[2]

We hear all the time about time management but if we adopt Covey's terminology, maybe what we really should be talking about is 'time leadership'. In other words, having a plan or a goal in mind will always mean that your activity is focused in the right direction. Don't just launch into your inbox as if you're diving into a rugby scrum which you then don't emerge from until the last person has left the building. Start by setting yourself a goal or specific tasks to be achieved in the day, and then focus your activity on getting those tasks completed.

Being your own leader means being able to step back and see the bigger picture. I believe this is one of the distinguishing marks between a good lawyer and a great lawyer. I remember one case I inherited where two opposing solicitors had written correspondence to each other on a single issue of whether a one-line letter was 'without prejudice' or 'open'. They had debated the case law in depth but the client had spent a fortune for two solicitors to engage in an academic debate – all of which was well researched and very eloquent, but utterly pointless.

Being your own leader, and therefore a great lawyer, involves a level of self-awareness. It involves the ability to question the direction in which events are going and to steer them another way. Lawyers must be concerned with detail. That's part of your job. So I'm not saying ignore the small print and fixate on the wider perspective, but get a balance. Learn how to step back and plan your time so that it is dedicated to the furthering of your goals, not anybody else's. By planning, you ensure that your time is spent on achieving results or furthering an objective, instead of just being busy.

Control time, don't let it control you

Making a plan is more than having a checklist of what you need to do. It enables you to retain control over your time. One of the main reasons time is wasted is that your time is hijacked by others as you go through your day. Interruptions, competing appointments, and distractions will all, without a plan, steer you off course and mean that you will be fully occupied but end up somewhere completely different to where you intended to be. Having a plan in mind, or even written down, will ensure that you remain focused on what you have to achieve in a day.

Your daily template

Alec Mackenzie advocates using a daily plan from which you can create an 'ideal day'.[3] Mackenzie writes: 'A daily plan, in writing is *the single* most effective time management strategy, yet not one person in ten does it.'[4]

It is important that any planning takes account of your energy levels and scheduled appointments. A daily plan is a regular routine where tasks are scheduled according to your needs and ability to concentrate. Many of us focus better in the morning and are less productive as the day goes on. I have always preferred a working template which means that I clear any intensive work at the beginning of the day and am able to deal with more routine work as the day goes on.

Of course, not every day will be the same. Depending on your area of expertise, you may say that no two days are the same, making it impossible to plan in advance. The point here is to have a basic structure which is flexible. If your supervisor schedules a conference at 5pm I wouldn't recommend you say that you are unavailable because that is your reading time. But, having a basic template for the types of tasks you are going to carry out at set times of the day will help you start from a more stable platform. When things do then crop up as they inevitably do, you are more able to fit them in.

To give you an example, the following model is an adaptation of Mackenzie's model to show how such a routine can be applied to lawyers' work. This is just an example. Your 'ideal day' can, and should, be very personal to you and should reflect how you work best. You will also notice that emails and phone calls are batched together (more on this in Chapter 7).

Some quick planning tips

The following are easy-to-follow planning tips:

- If you commute to work, instead of spending that time worrying about all of the things on your desk, spend that time mentally planning how you intend to spend your day and what you will have achieved by the end of it. Write it down if you're able to. What do you want to accomplish by the time you leave the office and which tasks do you wish to have completed?

Time	Task
8.30 – 9.30am	'Concentration time' – time for uninterrupted concentrated reading, drafting, or research.
9.30 – 10.00am	Read incoming post/check email. Plan morning's work.
10.00 – 11.45am	Client or internal meeting, or uninterrupted time devoted to one case or one intensive task, e.g. drafting a witness statement, reviewing a file, and preparing a report, etc.
11.45 – 12.30pm	Check email and return phone calls. Plan afternoon.
12.30 – 1.30pm	Lunch
1.30 – 2.00pm	Routine correspondence
2.00 – 4.00pm	Uninterrupted time devoted to one or more cases in turn or to in-depth tasks, or scheduled appointments such as client or colleague meetings.
4.00 – 4.45pm	Check email/return phone calls and diary actions.
4.45 – 5.30pm	Sign any post, carry out any marketing or networking tasks, read any journal articles you've flagged up, and prepare for tomorrow.

Table 1: Planning your 'ideal day'

- If you have a feeling of overwhelm, clear your desk of everything but one piece of paper. Map out what your priorities are and what you need to fit into your day. Only return those things to your desk which are part of that plan.
- Set time aside. If you are planning on a task which will take a set amount of time, book an appointment with yourself. Enter it into your diary as a meeting and stick to it.
- Set yourself a time limit. Parkinson's law says that work expands to fit the time available (which is why we are all super-efficient in the week before we go on holiday). Set yourself a window in which to complete a task and stick to it.
- Don't rely on your memory to follow-up calls, or chase colleagues or contacts, or to remember long-term tasks. Schedule such things into your diary. Schedule in reminders for follow-up actions.
- If you need to write an article, enter a diary reminder in advance giving yourself plenty of warning, then schedule some time in your diary to write it.
- At the end of the day, allocate the last five minutes to mentally list those tasks you have completed. Run through your achievements to remind yourself what you've been able to accomplish in a day, to put you in a better frame of mind and to enable you to switch off. If you wish, spend your last five minutes in the office also preparing a quick daily plan for the next day. You will be able to leave the office feeling more in control and will be geared up to launch straight into meaningful work when you return.

References

1. Covey, S.R., *The 7 Habits of Highly Effective People*, Simon & Schuster UK Ltd, 2004, p98.
2. Covey, ibid, p101.
3. Mackenzie, A., *The Time Trap*, 3rd ed. Amacom, 1997, p43.
4. Mackenzie, ibid, p45.

Chapter 4: How to prioritise

'One cannot manage too many affairs: like pumpkins in the water, one pops up while you try to hold down the other.'

Chinese proverb

As we discussed in the previous chapter, planning means taking control of your time. Prioritisation means choosing to spend that time on a piece of work according to its value. The operative word here is choice. How you spend your time is entirely your choice. It is entirely within your control. Anyone who says, 'I ran out of time' really means 'I prioritised wrongly'. As the proverb above eloquently illustrates, choosing to work on one task means you must deprive yourself of the opportunity to work on another.

Dealing with overwhelm

Many lawyers will be familiar with the experience of leaving the office knowing that they have been frantically busy all day, but feeling that they have achieved absolutely nothing. Perhaps you leave work feeling that you have merely scratched the surface, despite working at full steam all morning and afternoon. You will, therefore, feel exhausted after a long day of frenetic activity, but will feel despondent and disheartened thinking about what's left still to be done. The result is a huge effort in return for feelings of failure and defeat.

Turn your 'to-do' list into a 'to-day' list

One of the main reasons for such feelings of failure is the unsuspecting 'to-do' list. If you're feeling pressured and out of control, chances are you will make a list of all the things on your mind which you have to do. Your list might include routine items of correspondence, bigger drafting or reviewing jobs, perhaps some research that has been hanging around for a while, filling in your annual review form and returning it to HR, billing, reading the journal that came in last week, and so on. But, whatever is on your list, it is guaranteed to be long.

The problem is your daily to-do list contains far more than you could ever achieve in one day, so no matter how much you manage to get done, you will always end the day looking at a part-completed list, focusing on what you haven't done, and feeling defeated. I know more than one lawyer who keeps a to-do list on their PC, and who prints it off at the start of each day. What a way to ruin your morning.

If this is sounding familiar, here's what you do: by all means make your to-do list, but then edit it. Create a 'to-day' list – a list of only those things which can be done today. It might look something like the following:

- Task one – Respond to the letter from Smith & Brown solicitors;
- Task two – Complete annual review form and return to HR;
- Task three – Review list of documents drafted by trainee and send to client; and
- Task four – Complete letter of advice to client started last week.

Using the daily planner in Chapter 3, it now becomes easy to see exactly what you are going to do and when. What's important is that your 'to-day' list must be realistic and attainable. Once you've decided on your 'to-day' jobs, everything that is not for today must be put out of your mind or off your desk, so that you are not distracted by matters which don't need your attention yet.

At the end of the day, looking back at a completed schedule is far more satisfying than dwelling on what has yet to be done. And if you work through your 'to-day' list and do a bit extra, that's a bonus.

What's great about using a 'to-day' list and the ideal day planner is that you see the window of time as finite and then decide what you are going to do within it, as opposed to the instinctive reaction of seeing a list of tasks and trying to figure out how you're going to fit them all in. The truth is you will never fit them all in. As the famous saying goes, 'When you die, your inbox won't be empty'.

Where do I start?

The 'to-day' list will help if you are feeling overwhelmed and at a loss as to where to begin, but it won't help you determine what will be the most valuable use of your time. There are numerous tools out there which purport to teach the art of prioritisation. To my mind however, the key to a great time management tool is that it is quick and easy to use. What's the point in having to spend precious time scientifically analysing the pros and cons of where to start? Any sort of involved time management approach is definitely not going to work for lawyers.

	Urgent	**Not urgent**
Important	*The fire-fighter* Deals with crises and deadline activities such as last-minute court directions or meeting completion dates	*The effective lawyer* Occupied with crisis avoidance or preparation, case planning, marketing and know-how, client relationship building, health and wellbeing
Not important	*The easily-distracted* Reacts to interruptions such as certain client calls and emails, meetings and certain colleague discussions	*The procrastinator* Loses time on inconsequential email or phone calls, web surfing and other time-wasting activities

Table 1: How the matrix might look for a lawyer

The ABC approach

A well-known and very basic time management tool is credited to Brian Tracy and it can easily be adapted for use by lawyers. I call it the 'ABC of prioritisation'. It's about as straightforward as you can get and a good exercise for those moments when stress is preventing you from looking at your workload rationally.

Go through your to-do list and categorise items as follows:

A: Absolutely must get done today without fail – top priority;

B: Best if done today, but not as urgent as As;

C: Could do it today, but the world won't end if I put it off until tomorrow;

D: Delegate – this could be done by someone else, it doesn't need me; and

E: Eliminate – this doesn't need doing at all.

Once you've marked up each item, you pass the Ds to someone else such as your secretary, a virtual assistant, paralegal, or trainee, and the Es disappear. Then, work your way through the As, Bs, and Cs. It's that simple. This exercise is great for being able to weed out those tasks you don't need to do, instantly reducing your workload.

The urgent/important matrix

The problem with such a very basic time management exercise is that it's great for getting you back in control, but to really be effective, you need to consider whether you are allocating importance to tasks justifiably.

A more advanced time management tool is a well-known matrix which, although it has been around a while, may be new to many lawyers. The basic premise is that 'urgent' does not mean the same as 'important'. Just because something appears to have urgency attached to it does not mean that it is a valuable use of your time.

The matrix is set out in Covey's book[1] showing that we use our time in four ways:

- On things which are urgent but not important;
- On things which are urgent and important;
- On things which are not urgent and not important; and
- On things which are not urgent and important.

Urgent tasks will fight for your attention. A court deadline or completion date is hopefully very visible to you, which will mean that you will focus on meeting it. But in the same way, an incoming email alert will have the appearance of urgency – it flashes up on your screen and says 'stop what you are doing and read me now', but it is often unimportant. How many times have you interrupted an important drafting exercise to read a piece of spam email?

A successful and non-stressed lawyer would be living in the top right-hand box of Table 1 for as much of the time as possible. Jenny Ditzler calls this box 'Gold Time'.[2] If you are spending your days fire-fighting, you are reacting to urgencies. To exist in the top right-hand box you should be working on what is important but may not necessarily be demanding your attention.

Maximum results for minimum effort

Also known as the 80/20 rule, there is a principle originating from economist Vilfredo Pareto (who noted that 80 per cent of Italy's wealth belonged to only 20 per cent of the population) that 80 per cent of results are produced by 20 per cent of input or effort. The corollary is that 80 per cent of the effort goes only to producing 20 per cent of the results.

If you follow the Pareto principle, therefore, the key to effective prioritisation is focusing your efforts on the 20 per cent which will bring you the 80 per cent results. As Covey says, 'The key is not to prioritize what's on your schedule, but to schedule your priorities'.[3]

References

1. Covey, S.R., *The 7 Habits of Highly Effective People*, Simon & Schuster UK Ltd 2004, p151.
2. Ditzler, J., *Your Best Year Yet*, Harper Element, 2006, p163.
3. Covey, S.R., *The 7 Habits of Highly Effective People*, Simon & Schuster UK Ltd 2004, p161.

Chapter 5: The art of delegation

In researching this report I interviewed Sheenagh Parsons, managing partner at leading regional law firm, Attwaters. Sheenagh has recently taken a successful and busy law practice through a period of huge transition and re-branding, while maintaining her role as head of department and still managing a busy personal injury caseload. When I asked her how she did it, she summed up in one word: 'Delegation'. She explained: 'The art of wearing so many hats is learning how to delegate, not thinking you are the only person who can do it all. It's about learning to let go. We as lawyers take everything so personally. We tend to think we are the only people capable of doing things properly. Even now I still find it difficult to let go, but letting go enables me to do something else. It took me a while to learn that.'

The concept of balancing different roles is not the exclusive territory of managers and partners. All lawyers must adopt different roles, from being the adviser to the business person and from the accountant to the strategist. These comments sum up the difficulties lawyers face in delegating. Think back to the pumpkin proverb at the beginning of Chapter 4. While keeping one pumpkin underwater the other one escapes, but by deliberately releasing one, you can focus entirely on keeping the other firmly in hand.

Easier said than done

Lawyers are notoriously bad at delegation because it doesn't sit comfortably with the personal qualities which lead them to the profession in the first place. Many lawyers are born perfectionists and have an intrinsic belief that no one else could possibly do anything as well as, let alone, better than them. Many lawyers are control freaks, obsessive about detail, unable to trust others' contribution, sceptical, and demanding. While this sounds unappealing, many of these qualities have created some brilliant lawyers. The result is, however, that for many lawyers, delegation feels unnatural. By learning the art of delegation – a skill which must be learned and practised – you can increase your effectiveness, better manage your time, and reduce the pressure and stress you work under.

How to delegate properly

The great thing about delegation is that it buys you more time. However you slice it, you will only ever have a finite amount of time. By delegating, you instantly increase the number of hours available to you to accomplish what you need.

But delegation goes beyond this. It develops people and helps train staff. It is a vehicle for personal development, allowing junior staff to grow and take on more responsibility. As a result, it is also a powerful motivator. Effective delegation is actually crucial to everyone's progression. It allows you to train up successors and this allows you, in turn, to move forward. If you think of yourself as moving forwards when you delegate, the whole process will seem more positive and comfortable.

All of this does, of course, depend on doing it correctly. Not delegating at all, or worse still, delegating badly, will make you frustrated and stressed, and will cause other staff to be de-motivated and unhappy. Ineffective delegation means wasted time and resources, and leaves all parties feeling under pressure and unfulfilled.

Delegation and supervision – achieving a balance

I recall one partner who had a reputation for commandeering his assistants to sit in his office while he explained a task to them, and then made them sit there while he dictated a memo saying exactly the same thing. He would require his assistants to sit in on client meetings but would then have them be an audience while he dictated follow-up notes or letters. The result was a high turnover of juniors.

As a junior lawyer, I and my colleagues were endlessly frustrated when letters we had prepared were rewritten with amendments which were matters of style and not substance. Sometimes, it seemed that even the most mundane of correspondence needed three or four drafts before being released to the post room.

Of course, we must have training and learning. I would certainly never devalue these. To a certain extent, lawyers are caught between a rock and a hard place – the effectiveness of delegation versus the requirement of supervision. However, it is entirely possible to check work of assistants thoroughly without re-doing it, and that's where many lawyers are going wrong. One lawyer I spoke to said that she learned this sharply when she moved from a city firm where supervision was overbearing, to a regional firm where she was largely unsupervised. 'I learned more in the first month at my new firm than I had in the previous five years', she said.

There is no doubt that there must be supervision. The question is how can we make more use of delegation without compromising our professional standards?

The seven deadly sins of delegation

The following are the seven most common ways in which delegation can go wrong.

The need to control

A real issue for lawyers is the perception that delegation equals loss of control. However, delegation need not mean letting go of the reins. In fact, the key to successful delegation is to pass authority to others while maintaining overall control. By empowering others to make informed decisions, you are able to exercise greater control over a wider area. Think of delegation as controlling vicariously.

'It's quicker just to do it myself'

Another issue for lawyers is time. Many take the view that it will be quicker just to do the task themselves. In the time it has taken you to explain it, the task could have been completed. This is, of course, a very short-sighted view. Taking the time now to explain it properly means you have empowered a member of staff to do that task not just once, but always.

If you want something done properly, do it yourself

Lawyers can find it difficult to accept anything which does not meet their impossible standards. A concept lawyers are familiar with is 'fitness for purpose'. Try applying this to delegation. When you delegate a task, it does not need to be done as you would have done it. Don't assess the completed work by comparing it to what you would have produced yourself. Instead, judge it on whether it is fit for purpose. A good friend of mine, Heather Townsend (founder of consultancy The Efficiency Coach and networking group The Executive Village) regularly reminds her clients that when delegating, focus on results not method.

The 'I know best' syndrome

Confidence in one's ability and knowledge is an essential part of being a lawyer, but this can prevent lawyers from having faith in the qualifications of others. Accept that your colleagues have different information and qualifications which will inform and enhance the completion of a task. Sometimes, others will be better informed and qualified to do a job than you. For example, do not underestimate the knowledge a paralegal may have of the finer workings of a photocopier. I once had a superb assistant who could turn around a printing job in a fraction of the time I could have attempted it, and it looked better presented. Why would you spend your time on admin tasks when you have personnel who are better equipped to do them?

Keep your nose out

I have witnessed several lawyers labouring under the belief that they are delegating, but what they are in fact doing is assigning the job to someone else, then spending their whole time overseeing its completion. No one likes having someone look over their shoulder. If you delegate but retain too much involvement in the job, you're defeating the object. By all means be available for questions, feedback, and supervision, but limit that to specific times unless it's a real emergency.

'It's easier to do it myself'

If you think, it's easier to do it yourself, ask whether it is really easy for you to do it. Or, is carrying out the task causing you to feel pressure, making you overworked and resulting in you feeling stressed?

'I spent years mastering the task and I'm really good at it'

The temptation is to stay in one's comfort zone and to hang on to tasks which may well have taken you a while to master, but now that you are expert at them, you are quite happy tripping them out time after time. In law, it is important to learn the skills in the first place before you delegate them. Crucially, you must understand the legal principles and you can't delegate substantive work unless you know how to do it. But once you have mastered the basics, don't hang on to work just because it's easy or comfortable if it can be done by someone more junior.

Tips on delegating effectively

Plan it – identify who you're delegating to and when

In a law firm, this is likely to be a trainee, secretary, paralegal, or a more junior lawyer, but you may still need to give some thought to who is most suitable to carry out the work. It is a waste of resources to pass work to a fee earning member of staff if that work could properly be carried out by your support staff. I have come across partners who would often delegate to whoever was unlucky enough to walk through their door when they were looking at a particular case. Random delegation will de-motivate staff and will mean wasted resources.

It's also important to consider whether the work is of an appropriate level for the member of staff. Delegating work which is too senior, too demanding, or beyond a person's level of training will cause difficulties, including potential undesirable outcomes and a very stressed employee. Likewise, delegating a more basic task to a too senior employee will leave them feeling thoroughly unappreciated and undervalued. Think about the responsibility you are delegating, not just the task itself, and check with the other person that they are comfortable with this responsibility. You will, more often than not, be surprised to find that employees are capable of taking on more responsibility than you give them credit for.

Finally, don't dump work on someone just before a deadline because you didn't get round to doing it. Revisit the advice on planning in Chapter 3 and delegate well in advance. If you plan your own time and realise you won't be able to fit a task in, delegate it straight away so that your colleague can start working on it. Don't sit on it until the last moment, leaving someone else to work on the task under pressure and risk not doing it properly.

Explain the background

Think about the task from your colleague's point of view. What knowledge do they have? What will be obvious and what will you need to explain? In a legal practice, a delegated task will usually relate to a particular case or file. Take the time to sit down with your colleague and explain the background facts. This takes a bit of time, and this is the step which can put lawyers off (they think, 'By the time I've explained it, I could have done it myself – I know all about the file already'). But the time you spend explaining the context will save you hours in the future. Your colleague will then be fully briefed to take on any future tasks on the case, without needing you to explain things again. If it's long or complicated, build in time for them to read the file when setting deadlines, and encourage them to read the papers.

Explaining the background and how a job fits into an overall case plan or larger project is important training. It aids understanding in your staff and it will help them feel part of the team.

Give clear instructions

Once you have explained the background, give clear and simple instructions on what needs to be done. If you leave your colleague confused about what they are supposed to be doing, the task won't get done and you will have wasted time delegating it. You cannot be criticised for being too straightforward, but you will end up with difficulties for being too obtuse.

Also, be clear on the extent of responsibility being delegated. Asking someone to follow a set of instructions precisely to the letter is not delegation at all – it's instruction. Delegation involves the passing on of some responsibility for the task which will need to be carefully explained.

If you find you are delegating similar tasks periodically to different people, for example, explaining to trainees how to create 'lists of documents', think about devising a fact sheet. A help sheet will provide basic information quickly and will avoid the need for you to repeat yourself over and over.

Explain what the outcome should be

Discuss what you are expecting the completed task to look like. This ensures your colleague is working to the same expectations.

Check understanding and methods

Ask questions to check your colleague has understood what is being required of them. Also, check they are comfortable with the level of authority being delegated. If they feel uncomfortable with the task, they are likely to procrastinate over it and waste time.

Check how your colleague is planning to go about the task. In this process, encourage them to express their own ideas. Try to avoid being too prescriptive about how they do the task – this should be their choice. Allowing staff to select their own methods allows them to learn and develop, and empowers them in carrying out the work. If the task involves more than one component, talk about the priorities.

Set a timescale

When setting deadlines for delegated tasks, make sure you allow yourself enough time for review, amendments, and feedback, but make sure these deadlines are realistic. Don't set short deadlines if this is unnecessary. There is nothing more soul-destroying for a junior lawyer than a partner asking for a report in a very short time scale, who then allows it to sit on their desk for a week before they look at it. If the task is a long-term one, schedule in review meetings or conversations to check on progress or to deal with queries. A good tip is to schedule follow-up conversations when you first delegate a job. If you have set your colleague a deadline, make a diary note to speak to them before that day to check how they are progressing. Just a 'how's it coming along' conversation will reassure them that the job they are doing is not an unimportant one that you have dumped on them and forgotten about.

Ongoing support

It's a common problem that lawyers are left to get on with it – the 'don't come back to me until you've sorted it' philosophy. It's important to be available for colleagues to discuss problems or raise queries as the task develops. This needn't burden you with constant interruptions. If necessary, set aside specific times for staff to come to you with questions. Also, if there are overall developments in a case or if events take an unexpected turn, notify your juniors as soon as you can. If you leave a trainee drafting a witness statement when the case has settled, they will feel useless and de-motivated. Keep them appraised and they will feel an important part of the team.

Feedback

Let staff know how they are getting on as the task progresses, not just at the end. This should fall in naturally if you support and communicate as previously discussed, but it is vital to review the outcome when the task is complete. For trainees, in particular those in larger firms who carry out tasks for various supervisors, it is a common problem that work is done and returned and that's the last they hear of it. Giving comments and feedback will not just motivate and develop your staff, but it will ensure that tasks are improved upon every time.

Don't blame juniors if things go wrong

The worry of things going wrong is often what prevents lawyers from delegating in the first place. An undesired outcome in law can have catastrophic results. If you have followed the steps previously described, you should have sufficiently clear communication and understanding to ensure that you retain control over the overall process. However, it is important to understand that if you delegate, you still retain overall responsibility. The key to successful delegation is allowing sufficient freedom and empowering, while retaining supervision and control. It's a lot more difficult than you'd think, but it can be mastered.

The whole point of delegation is that it should free you up to devote more time to the high-value tasks (see previous chapter on how to prioritise tasks). Successful delegation can feel very liberating and can relieve you of a significant workload which, in turn, aids with stress. Delegation becomes more of a hindrance than a help when it is not done properly. If you invest a small amount of time ensuring conscientious delegation, you will reap the benefits. Delegating responsibility and devolving trust in your staff will lead to your own personal development and a more motivated and productive team.

Chapter 6: Procrastination – The thief of time

'Nothing is so fatiguing as the eternal hanging on of an uncompleted task.'
William James

In Chapter 4 we examined prioritisation, but there is a difference between identifying what your number one priority is and then actually doing it first.

Procrastination – or the putting off of important tasks – is a problem which plagues many lawyers. Given that lawyers charge by the hour, you would think they'd be less inclined to allow procrastination to happen.

Why do we procrastinate?

Putting off starting a task is not unusual, but why do so many lawyers do it? It seems straightforward to plan to start a task at 9am, but how many lawyers find it's 11.30am and all that's been accomplished is reading random emails and an interesting, but entirely irrelevant, article on your favourite website.

There are all sorts of reasons for procrastination. The fear of failure, such as worrying that one's work will be judged unfavourably or worrying that one's skills are insufficient, is a common reason, although there is also such a thing as fear of succeeding. Sometimes procrastination can result from disinterest, lethargy, or by a subconscious wish to sabotage the work.

Beating procrastination

Analyse it

To conquer procrastination, you have to recognise it. This is not as easy as it sounds. Putting off certain tasks could also be described as effective prioritisation. There is a difference, however.

If you read any general time management manual, one of the first things it will tell you is that to improve your time management, you have to first identify where you are losing time. Almost every time management book will suggest that first, you should record your time in order to identify how much time you are spending on various tasks.

You will already see where I am going with this. Lawyers have a distinct advantage in being able to recognise where they are losing time. Time recording for most lawyers is second nature. So, in theory, you're already half-way there. In order to get paid, more often than not, you have to record how you spend your time and you have to account for hours and even minutes. It should, therefore, be relatively easy for lawyers to be able to look at how much time they spend at work, how much they are billing for, and to work out the difference. The remainder is time spent on business development, doing admin tasks, or keeping on top of professional knowledge – or procrastinating. The amount of time you are not billing is basically time thrown away.

Recognise it

Procrastination is not only ineffective and delaying, but it results in stress, guilt, and feelings of failure which, in turn, cause more procrastination. Like many stress-related behaviours, it's a vicious circle.

To recognise procrastination when it's happening, the following are some common activities which should ring alarm bells.

The 'I'll just...' philosophy

Before you start a task, you'll make a coffee or you'll quickly send an email. Why not just do the task you're delaying? Give yourself extra motivation by allowing yourself a reward if you finish the task first. Once you've done this a few times, the feeling of accomplishment when you have achieved the task will be the reward in itself.

'I work better under pressure'

How many times have you said or heard this? The idea of working better under pressure is a myth. All that is ever achieved under pressure is the best you can do in the circumstances. Think about how much better your performance would be if you took the additional time to prepare and complete the task in good time.

Saved by the bell

Another common tactic is to allow minor interruptions to delay a more major task. Returning a quick phone call or email will seem like an ideal way of avoiding a more intensive task, and you can justify it to yourself by arguing that you are taking care of a seemingly urgent message. But, before you know it, you're caught up in a string of calls or answering emails and it's lunchtime before you've even thought about beginning the most important job of the day. You might persuade yourself that you're prioritising, but what you're actually undertaking is a form of displacement activity.

If you are prone to succumbing to interruptions, delay switching on your email until you've completed your first task, so that it's done before you get distracted. Leave a message on your email and voicemail to say that you are unavailable for a period of time to give yourself a window without interruptions (more tips on managing interruptions can be found in Chapter 7).

'I'll worry about it tomorrow'

You might think that you can forget about an important task until tomorrow, but in fact, it will still be on your mind and cause you some latent stress and worry.

Ostrich behaviour

This is where you ignore the task in the hope that it will go away or someone else will do it. If you are overwhelmed by a big task, break it down into smaller chunks with individual deadlines to make it more manageable. Do the most difficult jobs first to get them out of the way.

'I'm just too busy to do it right now'

Telling yourself that you are too busy to do something important amounts to bad prioritisation. You are busying yourself with less important tasks to avoid a more important one. Book the time needed for the task in your diary. Treat it like a meeting with yourself and take yourself to a different room or office if you need to.

Groundhog Day

It is counterproductive to write the same tasks on a new to-do list on more than one occasion. By all means have one to-do list, that's good time management, but spend the time you devote to writing additional unnecessary lists on completing the actual work.

Similarly, reading an instruction, letter, email, or diary note several times without actually taking any action relating to it is counterproductive. You might have been able to complete the task in the time you spent re-reading it.

File sorting

Tidying your desk, sorting out a file, looking for your highlighter pen, arranging your copies of the *Gazette* in date order, or any other similar activities will not get the job done and, more importantly, they are not billable.

Chapter 7: Managing communications and interruptions

Research carried out at Loughborough University showed that an office worker works three minutes before being interrupted by email, and it takes them 64 seconds to recover their train of thought.[1]

Gone are the days when, for a lawyer, dealing with correspondence meant opening the morning post and making sure anything which needed to be sent out in the evening's post was signed. In today's world, the array of communication methods available means two huge time management problems for lawyers – how to keep on top of incoming communications and how to deal with interruptions. Managing your email effectively will mean that you are better able to keep on top of the constant stream of incoming messages, without allowing emails to interrupt and divert your attention away from other work.

Nowadays, lawyers must keep on top of post, DX, faxes, emails, telephone calls, and even text messaging. Technological advancements mean that you are constantly reachable, but also constantly interruptible. It makes it more difficult than ever to focus on the task in hand and when it all gets too much, the internet offers you a convenient way of stepping out of your office – albeit virtually – offering you the ideal escape any time you like.

As methods of communication have evolved, so too have ways of dealing with them, and this has included the evolution of some very bad habits. Changing these can mean a much easier life. There are some very easy and effective systems or methods you can put in place which will help you manage your communications and instantly deliver more time for what's important.

Checking email

Checking email is the way most people habitually start their day. Is this necessary? No. Especially when it's likely that they checked it the moment before they left the office the previous evening. It actually means they are instantly diverted off course into dealing with other matters before they've even thought about how they intend to spend the morning.

The misconception many people have with email is that it should be an instantaneous form of communication. It isn't. For many, the thought of unopened mail in their inbox creates an uncontrollable urge to scroll through and open each new message to see what it's about.

Try this: introduce a new habit into your working day. Make your first task each morning a substantive task. In other words, when you sit down at your desk, do something which appears on your to-do list. Whether it takes 10 minutes or two hours, create a rule that you will not check your email until you have completed this task.

If this makes you feel anxious, imagine that you had an appointment first thing – you had to visit the doctor, take your mother to the airport, or go to a departmental meeting. If you had an appointment, you would not have checked your email until later.

Once you have completed your set task, take a break and then check your email. You shouldn't feel that you are on the back foot because you have checked your email later than usual. You should feel that you are already one step ahead, having ticked off one job from your to-do list before your day has really begun.

If you feel uncomfortable doing this every day, or if it isn't practical because of your client needs or the firm's policies on email, it is still a great way of motivating yourself to get through a particularly difficult task which is constantly being moved because you never manage to get started on it in the morning. Tell yourself that you're not going to switch on your email until you've completed the task. This ensures focus and it means once you've surfaced from your intense job, you can have some down time by checking your emails.

If this method works well for you, take it one step further. Once you've checked your email and prioritised your next job, switch off your email again until the next time you intend to check it.

Email notifications

I always keep these firmly switched off. I find it intensely distracting and irritating to receive a notification every time someone sends me an email. It compels you to check your inbox often only to find something inconsequential or spam. My own practice is to check emails three times a day: in the morning, around the middle of the day, and late in the day. If someone wants to get hold of you so urgently that they require an immediate response, they will phone – or they should. Too many people use email as a surreptitious way of attracting your attention when they don't feel able to pick up the phone and call. If it's really that urgent, they will phone and speak to you in person.

Some email tips

Automated e-mail responses

The most commonly used is your 'out of office' which automatically tells people you are away from your email. Most firms have a policy that you must switch these on if you are away from your email for more than half a day. But why stop at that? If you need a set amount of time to concentrate on a task, set your email to automatically respond with a message saying you're not available or 'away from your email'. Say what time you'll be back and give a phone number in case of genuinely urgent queries, then switch your email off or at least switch off any alerts, so that you are not tempted to look at new messages as they pop up.

Another practice I have come across is to set an automatic response to emails which says that the email has been safely received and you will respond as soon as you are able to. This is a great way of solving the problem of clients who email several times, then call you repeatedly to check you've received their email.

Checking versus actioning

Checking email often leads to dealing with it. It's tempting to fire off quick responses as you go along, or to be side tracked into a task you hadn't planned to deal with yet. If your emails contain larger, more substantive tasks, file them appropriately. If you can deal with emails quickly and immediately, then that's fine, but once you have done so, delete or file the email. Don't leave it cluttering your screen and making it look like you have more to do than you actually need to.

Don't deal with emails in order of your inbox. The time you received an email is not an indicator of its priority. Also, set a time limit for dealing with email.

Email rules and filing

Use email filters for filing emails which don't need to be read immediately. Set up folders for incoming newsletters so that those which don't need to be read urgently sit in allocated folders ready for when you have time for a catch-up session.

Spam and unnecessary email

If you are employed by a firm, your employer should have anti-spam protection in place. If you don't, you need to think about setting your spam filters. These are easy to do and will save you time. You do need to be careful that your filters are adjusted so that new genuine senders are not wrongly diverted.

If you receive newsletters, legal updates, or bulletins which you don't read or which aren't helpful, unsubscribe. Websites which send out useful bulletins will normally keep an archive which you can access when you need to search them for something specific.

Templates/standard emails

If you are sending similar emails often, create a template and save it in your drafts folder. For example, keep a template for an acknowledgement email in your drafts and cut and paste the wording each time you want to send a holding email.

If your firm doesn't do this for you automatically, set up an email signature and set your spell checker to automatically check emails before they are sent.

Holidays/out of the office

Finally, if you are going on holiday or are going to be away from your email for a significant length of time, leave an automated response saying so and give an alternative contact. This will mean that some queries may get sorted before you come back, lessening your workload on your return.

The internet

The internet is indispensable for most of us, but it can also be a giant plughole down which much of our time can disappear. Some firms restrict the use of the internet in any event, but if you do have free use of the internet while you work, you need to watch for time evaporating before your eyes. Use the internet for specific tasks, then shut it down the rest of the time. Do any drafting, writing, or concentrated work without going online to eliminate the temptation.

As discussed further in this book, social networking can be useful in terms of time-efficient business development, but social networking sites are dangerous – and not just from a time management point of view. These sites can eat up hours, but flippant remarks on a website can also get you into all sorts of trouble. Confidentiality is a huge issue for lawyers, so 'tweeting' absent-mindedly about your working day is best avoided.

There is, however, one very important time management implication I love about sites which require you to update your status. They make you think about how you've spent your time. If you find yourself struggling to sum up in 140 characters what you've achieved with your morning, then you haven't been spending your time effectively. Apart from that – treat 'tweets' with caution.

You can eliminate interruptions from the internet by managing your message-alert settings. Do you really need to be alerted every time you have a new follower on Twitter or someone posts a comment to a forum you have visited?

Telephones

Lawyers are traditionally taught to be available for client phone calls. Some firms do not employ secretaries so that lawyers take their own calls and they deliberately place an expectation on lawyers to answer client calls promptly and personally. I agree entirely that lawyers shouldn't hide in ivory towers but should be available to speak to clients when needed. However, I don't know if I subscribe to the view that lawyers should, or even can, take all calls at all times.

There's nothing to say you can't manage client telephone calls. You don't necessarily need to be available to answer all client phone calls instantly. I would even go as far as to say that sometimes, being too available can be counterproductive. It will simply encourage clients to call more frequently and, often, when it's not really necessary.

You do have a duty to your clients to be approachable and available, but you also have a duty to provide them with quality advice and legal representation – not something which is realistically achievable if you are always on the phone. You have a duty to provide considered and well thought out advice, which means you need thinking time. It just isn't realistic to think you can answer every phone call and deal with them instantly if you also have to devote time to drafting, negotiating, investigating, reading, researching, and all of the other things you have to do for clients.

Some telephone tricks

There are some simple but very effective functions available which, like with email, are underused. It's worth taking the time to see if you are using your telephone functions to their full capacity. If you don't have the technical knowledge or inclination to do this, commandeer a secretary or assistant or your firm's IT guru to help.

You should be using your voicemail to inform people when you're out of the office, but you can also use it if you intend not to answer the phone while you're focusing on a major task. It's easy to record a message saying you're unavailable for the morning, but will return the call in the afternoon. Always leave a number in case of emergency and if anyone really needs to get hold of you they can.

Never say in an email or phone message that you are away on holiday. I know of at least one professional who did this and then returned to find their house had been burgled.

Caller ID helps you screen your calls so you can allow non-urgent callers to be diverted to voicemail, and hands-free functions or headphones are a useful tool for lawyers. If you have a colleague working on a file with you, you can save time by inviting them to join calls. Get a junior to sit in on the call and prepare the attendance note. It also avoids spending time explaining what the call was about afterwards.

If you operate in an area of law which requires you to take comments on drafts, a great way of doing this is to invest in a set of headphones or an earpiece. Have your clients on the phone giving you their comments on a statement for example, while you simply type them in. It means you can finalise a document in a minimal number of drafts and avoid endless versions being circulated by email.

On a similar note, consider making a phone call instead of email from time to time and vice versa. If you are calling and never getting a response, don't waste time calling repeatedly. Send an email or other written communication asking for a call or dealing with the point. Alternatively, if it is something which can be dealt with quickly and efficiently by phone, why bother with a letter or email? Think about what you are trying to achieve, rather than creating communications for the sake of it.

Speed dial, storing numbers, and ring tones are all ways of saving you time. If you lack the enthusiasm to set these up, ask a secretary or support staff member to do it for you.

Prepare for longer phone calls by making sure you have everything you need to hand. If you are concerned about the call going off the beaten track, sometimes it's helpful to create an agenda and even send it to the other party before the call. This is especially helpful with clients who tend to stray off the subject and it's a good way of being able to reign them back in. It will help you avoid being stuck on the phone unnecessarily.

It's also a good idea to schedule longer calls. This enables you to ensure you have the time set aside to deal with them properly without feeling rushed. You can ensure you are not interrupted and it means the person you are talking to will also be prepared. You can also schedule an end time.

Exit strategies

A real problem is being kept on the phone unnecessarily. Have some stock phrases in mind which help you get out of an uncontrollable conversation. For example: 'I have an appointment in five minutes, so I'd better leave it there…' or 'I'd like to continue this conversation but…'

Stand up while you're on the phone. Being less comfortable will make you less inclined to keep the call going unnecessarily.

Colleagues and visitors

Open-door policies are something you'll often hear an enthusiastic HR officer promote as a defining characteristic of a firm's friendly culture. The phrase, 'And of course we have an open-door policy' makes me shudder slightly. More and more firms are now even going further and moving towards open-plan offices which makes the possibility of well-meaning colleagues interrupting you for a bit of friendly banter all the more likely.

Openness and accessibility to staff is one thing, but let it not be forgotten that lawyers often do complicated work and need to concentrate. What's so wrong about admitting that? We don't need to be constantly interruptible to colleagues. It is possible to have productive and rewarding working relationships without suffering constant unnecessary interruptions.

A good tip is to set aside a specific time for juniors to come and talk to you about a file. Conduct regular file reviews, which are best practice anyway, at which queries can be dealt with. Otherwise, ask them to book a time in your diary. This will ensure that your time is devoted to real queries of substance, rather than making it easier for your staff to pick your brains than think about a solution for themselves.

Is your desk positioned at an angle which invites visitors? Have you a chair next to your desk which makes it easy for visitors to come in and make themselves at home? Unless you need to see clients in your office, in which case it needs to be comfortable, think about how you are making it easy for staff to interrupt you. If you have a door, close it if you need some quiet time. It is possible to do this with an explanation to colleagues that you just need to work on something intensively for an hour or so. Of course, you need a balance. Make sure you open it when you're open for interruptions again. If you need some alone time, think about moving to a board room, the library, working from home, or whatever other option works with your employer.

A great tip a supervising partner taught me is to stand up when an unwelcome colleague enters your room. It is a surprisingly effective but subtle way of ensuring visitors won't stay too long.

Working from home

If you work from home you have a whole new set of distractions to deal with – TV, domestic chores, etc. If possible, have a space at home designated to work. If you don't have the space for this, you need to be disciplined with yourself. It can be tempting to think, 'I'll just get the dishes done before I start', but if you had to leave for the office, you would just let them wait until your return.

Mental distractions

Mental distractions shouldn't be underestimated and they can be exacerbated by stress, causing in extreme cases insomnia and other stress-related problems. Random thoughts of all the things you need to do can prevent you focusing on your work or getting to sleep. Keep a notepad and pen next to you and whenever random thoughts pop up, note them down. It's important not to action any of them, or to spend time making your list look nice or organising thoughts into different headings. Just get them down on paper so that they are no longer in your mind and can be organised or prioritised later.

Rewards

Finally, redefine your distractions. If you enjoy checking your online network, do it but use it as a reward to engage in once you have finished what you need to do. Set yourself a limit when you're on it but promise yourself another visit after you've completed your next job.

Reference

1. Jackson, T., *The E-mail Optimisation Toolkit*, ARK Group, 2009.

Chapter 8: Proactivity versus reactivity

'Reactive people are driven by feelings, by circumstances, by conditions, by the environment. Proactive people are driven by values – carefully thought about, selected and internalized values.'

Stephen R. Covey[1]

From what we have analysed so far, it can be said that time management is all about managing yourself. It's about being in control of your time. How you use your time is your choice. If you are overworked, stressed, unhappy in your profession, or are committing to things which are unreasonable or unnecessary, it's because you have chosen that situation.

The good news is that it is entirely possible to choose something different.

What do we mean by proactivity?

Being proactive does not mean saying 'yes' to everything, nor does it mean simply taking the initiative in the usual sense of the word. Being proactive means taking responsibility for yourself and electing how you intend to make the most of your time instead of allowing other people, events, or circumstances to dictate how your time is allocated. Being proactive means exercising self-awareness and will, rather than acting instinctively or through conditioning.

Being proactive means exercising self-discipline and self-respect. It means having respect for your time and recognising its value so that it is not wasted. As a result, you ensure that your time is spent on matters of substance which take you towards your goals. As the quotation at the start of this chapter teaches us, being proactive means acting in accordance with your internal values and not in response to external influences, meaning your actions have integrity.

It is important to read this chapter in the context of Chapter 3 on planning. Planning is about identifying your goals. Being proactive means acting in accordance with them.[2]

Identifying reactive behaviour

As we have explained in Chapter 6, to adopt a new behaviour, it is important to recognise when you are doing the opposite. Think about how you approach your work. Are you telling yourself the following:

- 'I hate that file. Something always goes wrong with it';
- 'I really have to call that client but I'm dreading the conversation';
- 'I'm so overworked, I can't cope with this many cases';
- 'Work is so busy at the moment I haven't even got time to take lunch';
- 'I just can't seem to get on top of things. I'll have to work all weekend to catch up';
- 'This client is so ungrateful'; or
- 'My supervising partner is so demanding'?

These are statements common to lawyers, but they are all examples of how we blame other people, things, or circumstances. They are examples of how we transfer responsibility elsewhere instead of taking control ourselves, and they are inevitably self-fulfilling. The more you tell yourself that you are stressed and can't cope, the more stressed and overwhelmed you will become. Alternatives might be:

- 'I am responsible for this file and I will choose a course of action in response to problems which arise';
- 'I can choose how I react to this client/request/instruction. My response is within my control'; and
- 'How I spend my time is up to me. I will consider the outcomes and make a choice'.

Setting boundaries

Setting boundaries for yourself is essential in a world where the legal profession is no longer just about advising clients. This can sound negative, as if it will lead you to make sacrifices or miss out on opportunities. Not so. The key is to set boundaries in accordance with your values and what is important to you, so that your actions are focused on the right tasks. Because boundaries are not often crossed blatantly, but are encroached upon gradually, it can be easy to find yourself in an unreasonable situation without really noticing.

Think of setting boundaries as identifying your values. For example, one of your core values might be spending time with your children. You might therefore deliberately choose not to work during weekends in order that you can focus on this value.

Learn how to say 'no' – or even 'maybe'

A key part of setting boundaries is to say no to certain demands. Saying no can be difficult for lawyers. Many believe that they must appear infallible, and to turn something down is to admit defeat. Others believe they can do everything. It can be very difficult to admit that some demands on your time are unreasonable or plain unnecessary.

For this reason, I think it is unhelpful to think of this concept as deciding what to say no to and instead, think of it as choosing what to say yes to. Again, you are saying yes to those things which fit within your frame of reference.

Part of the reactiveness we defined previously is an inability to stop and consider what your response will be, or even if a response is required. Sometimes you are saying 'yes' when what you really should be saying is 'no', or 'maybe', or 'let me think about that and I'll get back to you'.

In some circumstances, just deferring your response to give yourself time to think can be very valuable in allowing you to consider whether the demand is, in fact, a justified use of your time. So if you really struggle with an urge to enthusiastically agree to everything, give yourself a rule that your stock phrase from now will be, 'Let me just have a think about that and check my diary'. If someone asked you for money, you wouldn't just hand it over without question. Treat requests for your time in the same way.

Saying yes is often a short-term solution. Often, we say yes in order to please someone or rather, to not displease someone. Maybe we say yes because it seems too stressful or uncomfortable to say no, or because we feel guilty or responsible. What this leads to however is a situation where, if you say yes to everyone, you can't possibly get everything done. You're saving up problems for further down the line.

Think back to Chapter 5 on delegation and the 'it's easier to do it myself' theory. It might seem easier in the short term to say yes, but in fact, it could make life much more difficult for you further along. Consider also our pumpkin proverb. Remember that saying yes means that you will always have to sacrifice something else which won't get done. Whether this is other work, some free time, or time you would have spent doing something you enjoy. When saying yes, consider whether it's a fair trade off.

Saying 'no' to clients

How many things do you do for clients which aren't really necessary but which your client has talked you into doing, and which you agree to for a quiet life? Sometimes, what you should be doing is having that difficult conversation with your client to explain that you're not going to carry out their request because it's against your advice, unreasonable, unnecessary, disproportionate, or a waste of resources. If you're doing unnecessary work against your better judgement, are you really acting in your client's best interests? Here's how such a difficult conversation might go:

Client: 'I really feel like this claim is dragging. I'm feeling really stressed and anxious and just want it all resolved. I don't feel that anything is being done. Can't you just write a letter to the other side to put pressure on them to settle?'
You: 'I understand you feel extremely frustrated at the time it's taking to resolve this matter. Litigation can take a long time unfortunately. We could certainly send that sort of letter now if you wish. However, we've just recently made an offer of settlement which is under consideration. If we were to send another letter at this stage, it could undermine the strength of our negotiating position. My advice would be to hold off for a short time to see if we get a favourable response, but I do understand how stressful this must be for you.'

Sometimes, you need to say 'no' to clients. They may not like it and it may not be easy, but it is sometimes in their interests. Sometimes there is a positive duty to say no. You wouldn't advise a client to bring a case if it had no merits.

Saying 'no' to your opposition

How much of your time pressure comes from arbitrary deadlines set by the other side? When you're feeling under pressure, it can be easy to slip into complying with deadlines just to get them out of the way. Step back for a moment. Whose timetable are you working to? If you're in control of the case, it should be your own, not your opposition's.

Saying 'no' to colleagues

When you add your colleagues into the mix, you can see that there are demands being made on your time from all sides – clients, opposing parties, team members, supervisors, partners, junior staff reporting to you, external counsel, and so on. There aren't enough hours in your day for everyone.

It can be especially hard to say no to those you work alongside, whether it's those you report to or those you manage. It's crucial to allocate your time based on those who deserve it and not those who demand it. If you are struggling with management demands, consider allocating set times of the day when you will be available to junior colleagues. If you are overloaded with work from your supervising partner, be open with them about how much you have on your plate. They won't see you as incompetent. They will see you as someone who is serious about doing a good job and making the most of their working time.

Saying 'no' to yourself

By this, I mean consider what deadlines you are working to which are imposed by you alone. Are you feeling under pressure to get something done because you have promised something to a colleague or a client in an unreasonably short period of time?

The key is, of course, to set realistic time scales to begin with. If you are in a real fix, however, look at your deadlines and consider whether any can be deferred. People will often respond better if you call in advance, give them an update and explain that you need a little more time to do a job properly, than if you let the deadline pass and deliver work late.

References

1. Covey, S.R., *The 7 Habits of Highly Effective People*, Simon & Schuster UK Ltd, 2004, p72.
2. For practical ways to help you define your values and goals, read *Your Best Year Yet*, by Jenny Ditzler, Harper Element 2006.

Chapter 9:
Managing clients

How much time do you spend appeasing or avoiding clients who are chasing you? Lawyers have to take into account a variety of factors when prioritising, such as deadlines and client demands. Decisions on priority should not be made depending on who is shouting the loudest.

It's acceptable to have more than one client

There are plenty of lawyers who work on the principle that you should treat every client as if they are your only one. As a junior lawyer I recall being told that it was wrong to let on to clients that you have other files to work on and other clients to speak to. The mantra was always that clients should feel as if you are devoting all of your time and attention to them.

I'm expecting that some lawyers will disagree with me here, but in my opinion, this is precisely the type of approach which results in overwhelm and overwork. While there are some exceptions, in a large commercial law firm for example, it is entirely possible for a lawyer to have only one corporate client and their role is to ensure that this client is looked after at all times. However, it is perfectly acceptable to be open and honest with clients if you have other priorities and are busy with other matters. Clients don't (or at least they shouldn't) expect that theirs is your only case. You wouldn't visit a doctor, dentist, or any other type of professional and expect to be their only patient or client.

In fact, being in demand and having numerous clients gives the impression that your services are valued and popular. It shows your clients that you are successful and that others want to engage you. As a general rule, people will seek out lawyers who are capable, successful and, therefore, busy – not those who are struggling to get clients.

I would even go further and state that your practice depends on you having more than one client. If you didn't, your business would fail.

There's still room for quality

It is important to remember that the key is to manage numerous clients while still maintaining the same quality of service. If you have read the previous chapters, you will have realised that quality does not necessarily mean hours upon hours spent on a file. Quality of service comes from ensuring that your time is spent in a valued way. With that in mind, it is entirely possible to manage multiple clients while still delivering high-quality work.

Managing expectations

Managing clients and their expectations can be extraordinarily difficult, especially for trainees, newly qualified, or junior lawyers. It can be intimidating to have to manage clients who have had previous experience of instructing solicitors, because it requires self-confidence and sometimes assertiveness.

One of the most common mistakes is to agree to unrealistic deadlines with clients out of a short-term wish to appear impressive and efficient. What lawyers don't realise is that when you have to extend the deadline, or worse still, when you don't deliver on time and then avoid chasing phone calls, it creates a worse impression than if you'd estimated a longer lead time to begin with.

How many lawyers work with this thought process: 'I'll tell the client it will be done by tomorrow. They will go away happy knowing they have a super-efficient lawyer. I'll worry about how I'm actually going to fit it in later…'? Inevitably, this type of approach ends either with tasks not getting done on time or a very late night in the office.

It is important, therefore, to be realistic and honest with your clients. More often than not, your clients will be happy for you to take the necessary time to do a job properly, so set some achievable deadlines which you can stick to. Nothing impresses a client more than doing something when you said you would.

Keeping phone calls in check

As a lawyer it is possible to end up occupying the role of a counsellor, especially if you work in an area of law where clients are stressed, anxious, or are affected personally by the legal issue. As an employment lawyer I would often have the challenge of speaking to clients about harrowing and emotional experiences in their day-to-day lives. It is a real skill to be able to make clients feel that you are listening and understanding their problems, while still keeping them focused on the legal issues. I know many lawyers who are tremendously incisive and articulate but who, in their efforts to stick to the point, end up making clients feel that they are unsympathetic or uncaring. Striking the right balance is not easy.

It can feel unnatural for some lawyers to talk to clients openly about how they are feeling. It is effective to actually say to clients 'I understand' or 'I sympathise' or 'That must have been awful for you', but many lawyers find it difficult to say the words, preferring to stick to familiar legal territory. And this isn't really surprising given that the training offered to lawyers on how to deal with people is limited. It is better to constantly reassure clients that you understand their feelings, and in order to help them with their problem, you need to deal with a legal point. For example, saying, 'You must have had an awful time that day when that event happened. So, let's see how we can make sure we represent that in your case. Tell me…' This is a way of sensitively bringing clients back to the issue in hand.

Finally, clients with a pressing legal issue will naturally have that issue at the forefront of their minds and will be understandably anxious. If you deal with these types of clients, you might well arrive at the office to find several emails sent overnight and a voicemail waiting for you on your arrival to tell you that the emails are there. You may then receive a phone call at 9.01am asking if you've read them and what you think. Revisit Chapter 7 for how to deal with these problems. Perhaps, send a short message to confirm that the emails have been received and are receiving attention. In some circumstances, you are within your rights to kindly explain that repeated calls are not necessary. However, above all, the key is to strike a balance between reassuring clients that you are devoting time and attention to their case, while being able to convey to them that, in order to do this properly, you need to have time to read, digest, and process information.

Chapter 10: Networking and business development quick wins

One of the biggest challenges for lawyers is how to fit business development and marketing activities into an already busy schedule. Often, practice development can appear low on a lawyer's list of priorities meaning that less time is devoted to it. While this has short-term appeal, it can have longer-term disadvantages. Part of the secret to business development is maintaining a steady strategy. Having said that, there are some quick ways to achieve relatively short-term results. Different methods of marketing and networking work for different people, but this chapter introduces you to some of the most popular ways of getting some quick business wins.

Have a plan

We've discussed planning and its value in ensuring that you allocate your time in the most productive ways in Chapter 3. The same applies to marketing. It needn't be complicated. Just as you rely on a business plan, all firms should have a marketing strategy, which as a minimum, should cover some main areas:

- Target clients and areas of law;
- Methods of advertising or marketing;
- Budget;
- Time frames; and
- Methods of monitoring results.

Having this written down and noted on an appropriate partnership, board of directors, or management meeting agenda at regular intervals, will ensure that it is discussed and reviewed periodically and will keep the activities of relevant parties focused.

In larger firms, you would expect to see departmental marketing plans and it is even possible for individuals to draw up their own personal marketing plans (which can be done as part of an annual review process or separately). It's a great way for motivating individual fee earners, charting progress, and giving business development activities meaning.

Marketing – you're already doing it

Many lawyers think that devising a marketing plan means starting with a blank page, so this gets put off indefinitely.

You are already marketing without realising it. Everything you do day in, day out is an advertisement. Client referrals are a very powerful way of developing business. By providing an efficient, high-quality service to your clients, you are your best advertisement. So when you do a good job, make the most of it. Look for ways in which you can publicise your successes and achieve mileage from positive client feedback.

Use client feedback

Some firms send client questionnaires out to every client at the end of each matter. This is good practice as it will give you feedback on the level of service you are delivering. It means that you can use positive feedback in your marketing. Include in your questionnaire a tick box to allow clients to give their permission to their comments being used. If they agree, you can then instantly upload positive feedback onto your website or use it elsewhere. It's a quick way of building website content which is attractive and which many prospective clients will actually read.

Of course, if you use client questionnaires, you must also be prepared for any negative responses, but being alerted to them in this way means you are aware of any potential problems and are able to deal with them before they become bigger ones.

Updating your website

Having a website which can be regularly and efficiently updated is crucial. If your firm is big enough, you may have an individual with responsibility for updating the website. If you are a sole practitioner or with a small firm, you may pay an external consultant to help you or you may need to do it yourself.

Website design and maintenance is beyond the scope of this report, but if you are in a position where you look after your own website, you need to know that there are some fantastic services out there which provide you with low-cost (in some cases free) websites which give you total control of the editing, meaning you can access your website whenever you'd like to add content. Just adding positive client testimonials to your website makes a difference to its appeal.

Online networking

I have found this to be an effective and time-efficient way of networking. The main social networking sites (Twitter, Facebook, LinkedIn, and YouTube) are now being used cleverly by some lawyers, and they are leading to significant business and marketing opportunities.

In my view, online networking lends itself ideally to busy professionals. It may take a little bit of time to master the basics, to set up profiles and build networks, but once you have the fundamentals in place, it becomes a very efficient way to maintain a networking profile.

For those who have yet to discover these sites at all, the key to online marketing is that you update your status to broadcast what you're currently working on. This can be used for anything from social pleasantries, to highlighting a new article on your website, mentioning a seminar you are speaking at, or asking people to sign up to a newsletter – the possibilities are endless. The beauty of it is you are limited to a small amount of text you can post at any one time, so inherently you have to be brief.

It is also a good way of keeping in touch with people without having to send lengthy emails. If you haven't talked to someone in a while and send them an email, you feel obliged to make it substantive – which means you might end up putting it off. With social networking, you can send short updates to anyone you like, thereby keeping in regular contact and ensuring you are still at the forefront of their mind if they have a business referral. Online networking is also a great way for sharing legal information. What's more, the main networking sites are now constantly revising their service so that you can use tools to connect your different networks and publish information once to appear in several places and reach the maximum audience.

Finally, there are some interesting tools for monitoring the effectiveness of your online activity. They take a bit more study but they are ways of ensuring that your online networking time is working as hard as possible for you.

'Re-purposing'

I was introduced to this term by leadership coach Duncan Brodie and it is a clever way to describe how to get the most out of your marketing activities. Writing articles is a popular way for lawyers to gain exposure. With all of the methods of publication now available – firm websites, email newsletters, blogs, social networking sites, magazine websites – and that's just online, there is an opportunity for lawyers to re-purpose written material by adapting news articles or press releases to different media or outlets, so that maximum value is achieved out of your efforts. If you have invested a significant amount of time in producing an article or case report, think about how it can be adapted for other purposes. Can you use the content in a seminar or journal, for example?

Chapter 11: **Managing pressure and stress**

We are constantly reading reports about how stressed or unhappy lawyers are. Even as I began this chapter the *Law Society Gazette* landed on my doormat containing an article (8 October 2009) claiming lawyers are the most unhappy professionals. Take some of *The Times*' headlines in recent years: 'The stress of being a female lawyer' (30 July 2009), 'Long hours and stress drive lawyers to drink and drugs' (6 October 2008) and 'One in four lawyers wants to change jobs' (2 July 2007).

There's no denying the regular stream of surveys, articles, and reports which put lawyers at the top of the list for the most stressed out professionals, and since the economic downturn, reports have emerged about an increasing number of lawyers checking themselves into rehab with exhaustion.

But stress still has a stigma attached to it which prevents lawyers recognising and dealing with its symptoms. Lawyers are expected to be robust, tough, and emotionless. Admitting to stress simply does not go with the territory. The effects of stress are still being seen across the board with some lawyers turning to alcohol or drugs, some suffering relationship problems or divorce, and others deciding to leave the profession.

The bottom line is that stress is best dealt with early on – the sooner you see the signs and address them, the quicker you can revert to a balanced, happy, and productive working life – but the trend is for lawyers to let it fester until the effects are more serious. Lawyers will end up working long hours and taking little time to look after their wellbeing in an effort to keep on top of things, but this approach is making them more stressed and, as a result, less productive. We're back to the vicious circle illustrated in Figure 1, Chapter 1.

Alcohol and drugs

The charity LawCare was set up in 1997 originally to provide telephone support and counselling to lawyers suffering from alcohol abuse, although its mission statement is to offer support on any health issue. Now, it largely receives calls from lawyers, their staff, and their families, dealing with stress and depression. Anna Buttimore at LawCare said: 'What is interesting is that most callers wishing to discuss alcohol problems are partners, heads of chambers, or those who have been qualified for a long time. It seems that women are more able to talk about stress. We receive a lot of calls from newly qualified female lawyers talking about stress. Men, on the other hand, seem to turn to drink and they end up calling years later to discuss an alcohol problem.'

In his private practice, Dr Mike Drayton, a clinical psychologist with over 25 years' experience, regularly works with lawyers and his view is that stress is endemic in the legal profession. Dr Drayton is interested in working with lawyers because they are generally 'healthy, resilient, and psychologically robust people with precision of thinking', but he sees a strong connection with stress and alcohol. 'I don't think I've seen one stressed lawyer who was not drinking. Alcohol is self-medication for anxiety. It has fast-acting physiological effects which work quickly to calm you down at the end of a busy day.'

What can firms do about stress?

One difficulty with stress is that it can be caused by work or it can originate from personal problems, but often these are so interlinked that stress eats away at every area of life. Stress can result in employee absence and firms often don't know how to start addressing it.

In larger firms, responsibility for stress and wellbeing could be owned by any number of departments – HR, facilities, or learning and development. It is interesting that now certain firms are recognising mental health as an area in itself. Carolyn Lee is head of diversity and inclusion at Herbert Smith. Part of her remit is advising on the management of employee stress, mental health, and wellbeing, and she is a believer in confronting stress head-on: 'Stress is seen as a hot potato. Organisations are scared to discuss it because as soon as they discuss it, it becomes an issue.'

Herbert Smith, for example, carries out a biennial staff survey which, for the first time in 2007, contained questions about stress. The collapse of Lehman Brothers and its ripple effect across the City, led the firm to institute mental health awareness training.

Carolyn Lee said: 'At the start of the recession, our people were not under threat, but many of our staff were in relationships with employees of the banking sector, which meant that job certainty became a real worry for them as they found themselves being sole breadwinners. Our people were stressed. We took a big picture view. We wanted a course which was not "fluffy" but which would tackle and recognise stress. It was borne of a genuine willingness to help people. We worked with a psychotherapist and produced a guide for staff on understanding mental illness. Although the course was optional, around 230 employees – far more than we expected – have taken it up so far. One head of division told me it was the most useful course he had ever attended.'

What surprised me was the backlash experienced by the firm, from external critics who suggested that it was a cynically motivated measure to pacify professional indemnity insurers, amongst other things. So it seems that, to some extent, firms are damned if they do take action on stress and damned if they don't.

The economics of stress

In November 2009, the BBC reported that according to the National Institute for Health and Clinical Excellence (NICE), the national cost of work-related mental illness had now reached £28 billion. Over 13 million working days a year are lost due to work related stress, anxiety, and depression. And lawyers are not exempt.

In Dr Drayton's experience, most interventions with lawyers pay for themselves several times over, and that's just in terms of preventing lost billable hours. In one case, his intervention with an equity partner led to a financial saving for the firm of over £200,000. He is also of the view that a big key is realising that when working long hours towards the end of the day, lawyers are operating at maybe only 30 per cent efficiency. That can't be good for an individual or a firm. The simple practice of working shorter days actually increases productivity. It's also a client retention issue. Stressed lawyers inevitably damage the client relationship leading to less satisfied customers. Happy lawyers retain clients, simple as that.

Individual or cultural change?

LawCare's definition of stress is interesting: 'Stress is your reaction to the levels of pressure upon you.' It's true that stress can start to exhibit itself as a feeling of being overworked and under pressure, leading to feelings of tiredness and irritation. Stress then leads to unhealthy behaviours such as comfort eating, or turning to drink or drugs. The ultimate price is a complete mental or physical breakdown. But these arise because of one's reaction to one's circumstances, and that is something we have control over. Being stressed is a choice. It is a decision over which we can take responsibility. As soon as lawyers realise that they can make a decision not to be stressed, they often experience feelings of relief.

Dr Drayton told me that often, clients see him when they are stressed and he helps them to overcome this, but when they return to work, the problem will recur because the problem is not with the individual but in the culture. He told me that basic time management plays a big part in managing stress as does managing client expectations. He said: 'It is organisational cultures which need to be worked on, not individuals. Change needs to start at the top.'

Dr Drayton firmly advocates a work-life balance and confirms what was explained earlier in this report, it is essential to set boundaries. He has worked with City partners who sleep with their BlackBerries next to their beds. He routinely reminds his clients that lawyers are paid to think and it is impossible to do this when they are constantly being interrupted by emails. 'The problem is firms don't know how to support their employees. Often, they are well intentioned but they are at a loss as to where to start. When they get professionals involved, they are often psychiatrists not psychologists, and there are so many complex psychological variables.' Dr Drayton uses emotional intelligence as an approach, believing that the cause of stress is less relevant than helping people through it.

The answer seems to be lawyers (and particularly partners and those leading by example) taking individual responsibility for their own wellbeing, combined with a cultural shift to eliminate stress from the profession. I wonder whether one wouldn't result from the other. Carolyn Lee sums it up in this way: 'Firms know that [stress management] has long-term benefits, but they must develop a culture where this can be done. We have to recognise that there are some things we can't change, but we're trying to help people to help themselves.'

Chapter 12: Personal development and career planning

'Time = life; therefore waste your time and waste your life, or master your time and master your life'

Alan Lakein

In Chapter 3, the importance of planning and beginning with the end in mind was emphasised. This 'end' can be interpreted in many ways, and this type of planning can be applied on many levels. The end can mean the end of your hour-long task, the end of your week, year, or your life.

I recall vividly a speech given by the senior partner at a firm on his retirement day. He told of how he had spent 40 happy years at the same firm, in the very same office, and how quickly that had passed. A respected practitioner in his field and a highly regarded member of the legal community, this had been his ambition and his achievement.

At that moment, my entire working life flashed before my eyes. Could I see myself standing in this same building, in this same room, 40 years from now? I felt panicked at the thought. Not because I disliked my job, but because that wasn't necessarily my game plan. Well, in fact, I had no game plan. That was the point. In that moment I began to assess where my career was going. Did I want to become a partner in the City? Did I want to be a lawyer my whole life? What did I really want from my career and from my life? It wasn't that I realised I was necessarily on the wrong path, it was that I simply hadn't thought about it and it was frightening to realise that 40 years could pass before I had given it any consideration.

What I realised then, and what I am constantly reminded of since, is that many lawyers forget to take a moment to look up from their busy caseloads to think about the broader context.

Anthony Robbins, US life coach said: 'Once you have mastered time, you will understand how true it is that most people overestimate what they can accomplish in a year – and underestimate what they can achieve in a decade!'

Managing your time on a basic level means achieving your potential on an hourly, daily, weekly, and yearly level. Extending this through the long term means achieving your potential in life.

We have already seen how daily planning can ensure that your time is not hijacked by meaningless or unimportant activities. How much more important is this for life planning?

The importance of life planning

Many coaches carry out an exercise with clients where they will ask them to imagine listening to their own eulogy, or to imagine themselves at an awards ceremony at the end of their lives where they are to receive an award. What would they want to hear said about themselves? What achievements do they imagine being celebrated?

Considering the end of your life in this way means that you can identify what success means to you. Is it to make partner? Is it to earn a high salary? Is it to work for a charity? Is it to spend time with your family – or even to have a family? By knowing your own definition of success, your daily management of your life has purpose in moving you towards your goals.

Your values

You may or may not have been involved in business planning. If you have, you will know that most business plans contain a mission statement – a business philosophy. Identifying your values is like developing your own personal mission statement which reflects what is important to you and how you wish to live your life. It is a definition of your personal philosophy, a reminder which can be returned to any time you feel that life is out of control, when you feel in need of direction, or when you feel that you are falling into reactive behaviour.[1]

Not just a lawyer

At the beginning of this book, I acknowledged that practising law is not just a job, it is a professional vocation – a way of life.

Just as with other professions which involve a great deal of hard work and commitment, it is easy to feel that the title 'lawyer' is all and everything you are. It is your life's work. Many lawyers feel that, in order to succeed in the profession, they must invest heavily to the detriment of other areas of life. They balk at the idea of work-life balance, and many sacrifice family, spare time, outside interests, friends, health, and well-being for their work. With this outlook, it can be easy to react disproportionately when challenges appear on the professional horizon, but more critically, it can result in reaching the end of a legal career to find that other of life's territories have been left undiscovered.

Hopefully, this book will have prompted you to invest in the belief that a successful legal career and a healthy balanced life are not mutually exclusive. But even if this book has done nothing more than inspire you to think about how you use your time, that is one step closer to a more fulfilled career and a healthier legal profession.

Reference

1. For more on how to identify goals and values, read *Your Best Year Yet* by Jenny Ditzler, Harper Element 2006.

Chapter 13:
Practical examples

In this chapter, you'll find advice from some typically busy lawyers in private practice, who share their thoughts on how important good time management can be.

Example one – The managing partner

Sheenagh Parsons, managing partner, Attwaters Solicitors

It is important to have confidence in those around you. The key to delegation is delegating responsibility and accountability. I have a practice manager and a HR manager with whom I meet regularly. They keep me updated and I manage the process. My role is to drive the business forward in the way the partners decide they wish to take it. I have to make sure everyone else does their bit. If I were to get involved in carrying out everything which needs to be done, the whole process would fall apart. I have to keep an eye on the bigger picture and make sure the cogs are turning around as they should be.

There is an incredible squeeze on the profession nowadays. People feel pressurised not only in their daily work, but elsewhere. The culture creates pressure. Solicitors are traditionally bound up in a culture of doing long hours, and this causes junior fee earners to view long hours as the norm. It is important for fee earners to remember that we like to see staff working hard and achieving results, but working long hours is not an automatic indicator of either. Fee earners should focus on the end result. There is a misconception that if someone is working late in the office, they must be contributing a lot to the firm, but while we do want to see fee earners show us that they are prepared to go the extra mile (for example, through involvement in networking or marketing events), if someone is regularly working late in the office there could be something wrong. There are, of course, fee earners who work long hours to over achieve, but when long hours are combined with poor or mediocre performance, alarm bells should ring.

Time for proper consideration is vital. We tend not to think of thinking time as having any value. It is not considered to be an activity and we usually don't record it. It is hard to record this time even though it usually adds most value to a file.

It is important that fee earners learn about what they should and shouldn't do on a file. Tidiness does not necessarily mean that someone is being proactive on that file. It is easy to move paper around and to send a letter to show that a file has been worked on, but that action may not necessarily have taken the matter forward. The key is to do everything that needs to be done on that file so that progress is made. While there is an immediate short-term relief of pressure because you feel you have done something on the file, in reality, you could have done more and relieved a longer-term pressure.

Example two – The City partner

There is no doubt that there are enormous demands now on the profession. In today's legal market, we have to work very hard so as not to fall by the wayside. The easy answer to all of this is to work longer hours. The demands on managers are much greater than they used to be. Everything is constantly changing – the way we offer services, the way we address our competition, and so on. We can't afford to stand still. If we do, we will end up going backwards.

As a partner, I am the salesperson – the 'work-getter' – and I also have responsibility for quality control and recruiting the best people. At our firm, we have introduced a career framework to plot out career progression for everyone. It provides clear targets and an understanding of the benchmarks. Often, fee earners don't know what their expectations are. This new framework is challenging, but it allows assistants to see where they are and what they are aiming for. It makes fee earners more productive and motivated. I see the partnership model contracting. The percentage of partners is decreasing year on year. This structure allows us to train up our successors, who will ultimately relieve partners of service delivery and client management. Ultimately, it will free me up to carry out the business developer role.

The legal market has changed, and as a profession we have had to make ourselves incredibly efficient to compete. We have had to be creative and reinvent our offering, such as by devising new products. Our support teams have also developed to maximise efficiency. They are no longer managed by partners, but have their own specialist directors in those fields.

Balancing a legal career with family life is challenging. I couldn't do it if I didn't have a really stable family and home life. Now more than ever, I have to work long hours to keep on top of things – regularly over 10 hours a day. Yes, I'm tired but I made a rule early in my career that I would never work weekends. Weekends are my time for family. I make sure I sleep and I take time to walk or exercise and eat properly. It's important to keep rounded. Without this balance, it would be impossible for anyone to keep going.

Example three – The new partner

Madeline Seibert, partner, Attwaters Solicitors

After I had my daughter, I returned to work on a four-day week and I became partner earlier this year. I still have a feeling of guilt about working part time, even though I work from home most evenings. After a full day in the office, I usually start work at home at around 8.30pm and will normally work until 10.30pm or 11pm catching up on dictation, reading medical reports, or proofreading marketing newsletters. Since becoming a partner, there are more duties to fit in the working day – marketing, case reports, supervision, meetings – so when I arrive home, I have to catch up on chargeable hours. I feel that as a partner, I must set an example and although I have always made sure I meet my targets, now I feel a greater obligation because I cannot expect other fee earners to meet targets if I don't do it myself.

For female solicitors there is a huge conflict between career and family life. I have come a long way in my career and I certainly don't want to give up now. I still have much I want to achieve, but I also need to have a balance and be able to spend time with my daughter. I am very lucky to have my family around to help with childcare; however, whether or not to have a second child is still a real dilemma for me, as it must be for many other women in this position. Taking maternity leave would interrupt the momentum of my career, and on a day-to-day level, it would present huge challenges.

The only way I can keep on top of things is to be incredibly organised. My home and work life must operate to a tight routine and there is little room for manoeuvre. In the office, I plan work carefully and always operate with a list of jobs to be done. With the help of my secretary, I keep files organised. I couldn't operate in a state of chaos or untidiness like some lawyers do. For more concentrated work, such as drafting statements or reports, I do this at home where I can work without interruption. We do have firm-wide procedures and checks in place (such as matter lists to identify files which have not been worked on and central limitation records), but on top of this, I have my own systems and working habits, because time is like gold dust and it is crucial for me to squeeze as much as possible out of my day.

Example four – The assistant solicitor

James Woodhouse, solicitor, Charles Lucas & Marshall

As a trainee, prioritisation was really the key to successfully managing the workload. Communication with solicitors was essential to determine how much urgency should be attributed to a particular task. Now, I work more autonomously and I manage my own caseload which is a mixture of civil litigation and employment. To a certain extent, this is easier because I can organise my own time. My caseload demands that I keep a very close eye on deadlines. It can be stressful because you always worry about missing a deadline, but being organised and making sure my diary is up to date helps.

I am also lucky to have great secretarial support. I work across two teams so I have the benefit of working with more than one secretary. As a junior lawyer, it was daunting to delegate to staff who were more experienced than I am. I used to do a lot of the work myself until I became more confident and was able to delegate more. As you gain experience as a solicitor, your quality of work improves and you learn to make more use of the support available.

Timesheets are a struggle for most lawyers. Since qualifying as a solicitor, however, I have always had responsibility for meeting a fees target, so I have learned the value of accurately recording time. I now always prepare my own bills so I know that writing time off will impact on my billing figures. But it is also essential to balance this with client expectations. It can be incredibly difficult as a junior lawyer to deal with clients who are experienced in instructing lawyers. They may be comparing the service they are receiving to what they have experienced in the past from other more experienced lawyers. It can also be difficult to gauge what is a reasonable fee estimate when you have no experience of the work. This all comes with time.

Time management is important for me and I always try to do it intrinsically. It is also important that I have down time outside work, so that I can pursue all of my other interests. I am lucky to work in a firm where there is no culture of working long hours for the sake of it, so work-life balance is not an issue for me.

Example five – The trainees

The real estate trainee

We received formal training in time management as part of our training contract, and this has been of great value considering a lot of our work depends on billing effectively. It can be challenging to judge how to spend an appropriate amount of time on matters in order to make sure that no client is left out. In the real estate department, the workload is intensive. I have found that it is important to keep up the stamina without panicking.

I have always used lists to manage my time and I have continued using these since joining the profession. Also, delegating the administrative tasks to secretarial support staff has been a valuable lesson I have learnt and a skill which I am still trying to develop. I do work 10-hour days, but I have managed to strike a balance. I realised early on that, although others tend to prefer working later in the day, I work best in the mornings. This means that I then have the evenings to myself.

The corporate trainee

Time management is incredibly important in the corporate department as all work is performed to deadlines (whether statutory/contractual or set by the client) and you are often expected to juggle a varied caseload with a number of different deadlines. My main challenge is refusing to take on more work if I am already working at full capacity. But I have learned that it is important to be realistic about time frames and deadlines, and to notify the relevant person as soon as I become aware that I may not meet a deadline. I have also learned the benefit of making the most of my time during the quiet periods to carry out practice development work, for example.

Milton Keynes UK
Ingram Content Group UK Ltd.
UKHW022040280723
425987UK00010B/119

9 781906 355777